VEGETARIAN KETO
DIET COOKBOOK FOR BEGINNERS
2 IN 1:

To Help You Lose Weight Naturally With Tasty Seasonal Dishes That Will Boost Your Energy And Improve Your Life.

RIHANNA SMITH

THIS BOOK INCLUDES:

BOOK 1:

VEGETARIAN KETO DIET FOR BEGINNERS

A Detailed Cookbook with Delicious Recipes to Lose Weight Naturally with Tasty Seasonal Dishes and the Complete Guide to Always Stay Fit

BOOK 2:

KETO VEGETARIAN COOKBOOK

A Simple Cookbook to Change Eating Habits with Low Carb Recipes for Beginners and Plant Based Meals for Boosting Your Energy and Improving Your Life

VEGETARIAN KETO DIET FOR BEGINNERS

A Detailed Cookbook with Delicious Recipes to Lose Weight Naturally with Tasty Seasonal Dishes and the Complete Guide to Always Stay Fit

RIHANNA SMITH

TABLE OF CONTENCT

VEGETARIAN KETO DIET FOR BEGINNERS

Introduction

I n one form or another ketogenic, or keto, the diet has been in use for centuries. In ancient Greece, physicians treated various diseases, especially the disease of epilepsy, by making changes in their patient's diets. Many Greek physicians believed that there was a physical and rational basis to use dietary therapy to cure illnesses and conditions.

The first study of a modern type was not conducted until the twentieth century. A group of patients with epilepsy was treated with a vegetarian diet that was low in calories. Those who maintained strict adherence to the diet were able to greatly decrease or end their seizures. Scientists who studied the results of this experiment found that there were three compounds that are water soluble and are located in the liver of healthy people who were adhering to a very low calorie or a starvation diet. They coined the term 'ketone bodies' as a name to call these compounds. Other doctors built on this research and discovered that the body could be made to produce ketone bodies when it was fed a high fat low carbohydrate diet. Because of the ketone bodies, the term 'ketogenic' was first used.

The first keto diets varied widely in the ratio of fats to proteins consumed until a pediatrician tried using the diet on his patients to see if it could reduce or eliminate their symptoms of epilepsy. His formula was for the patient to consume only one gram of protein for every pound of body weight, fifteen to twenty grams of carbs per day, and the rest of the caloric intake would be made up of fat. Besides reducing the seizures of epilepsy doctors noted that their patients slept longer and more soundly, had an improved level of alertness, and experienced better overall behavior with very few or no side effects.

The keto diet was widely used as a treatment for epilepsy until the middle to the latter part of the twentieth century when anti-convulsing drugs became more readily available and highly popular. Taking a pill is much easier than sticking to a rigid diet. So, the keto diet fell out of favor until the 1990s, when a television producer and his wife were searching for a treatment for their young son, who suffered from debilitating seizures that even high doses of medicine did not stop. Their child did so well on the keto diet that they promoted it to everyone who would listen, and the diet was once again popular.

In normal physical processes, the human body will burn carbs for energy. The body turns carbs into sugar, or glucose, during the process of digestion.

When people eat the pancreas gets a signal from the brain to produce insulin to help take the sugar produced by digestion through the bloodstream and into the cells. The insulin is actually the key that gets the blood sugar into the cells. The pancreas will produce as much insulin as the body needs to transport and disperse the amount of blood sugar the body has to get rid of. The body will also store a precise amount of blood sugar in the liver in the form of glycogen. This is a type of emergency store in case the body faces starvation before the next meal appears.

The problem begins when there is too much blood sugar, as usually happens when people eat a high sugar high carb diet. Eventually, the cells will have all of the glucose that they need and they will begin to ignore the insulin when it comes knocking on the cell door. This is known as insulin resistance. The body then needs to find a place to put all of this excess glucose so it stores it as fat beginning around the organs of the abdomen and then spreading out to other areas of the body.

The predominant goal when following the keto diet is to lower the consumption of carbs enough to burn body fat enough to cause massive weight loss. The other part of that goal is to feel fewer food cravings, especially for sugary foods, while making the body feel full with less food consumed.

When the consumption of carbs is restricted to a low level the body needs to find a new source of energy for the cells to be able to function. The body will first begin to burn the glycogen that is stored in the liver when the supply of blood sugar in the bloodstream decreases. The liver can store enough glycogen to fuel the body for about forty-eight hours. After that time the body will search for other ways to obtain fuel for the body to use. The liver will use the stored fat in the body to break it down to make fuel.

Your body goes through a perfectly normal metabolic process called ketosis when it begins to burn stored fat for fuel. This is a perfectly normal process the body goes through when access to carbs is limited or eliminated. The body produces ketones when it goes into ketosis and this is what the body uses for fuel instead of carbs. This is a feature that was built into the body ages ago to keep early man from starving to death during times when food was not readily available.

Ketosis is the name given to the body's function of making ketones from stored fat for fuel for the body. The body will usually enter ketosis after about three or four days of eating a low carb diet. The main purpose of following the keto diet is to get the body to enter ketosis because this means the body has begun burning stored fat. Most people enter ketosis with few to no symptoms, and some people experience what is called the 'keto flu' because the symptoms feel much like having the flu.

During the beginning of ketosis, the person may experience very bad breath. This happens because the body is breaking down toxins with the breakdown of stored fat, and toxins are removed from the body in three ways—through urination, through sweating, and through the respiratory system.

So your body is sending out toxins with every exhale. This symptom will only last a few days, and more tooth brushing or use of mouthwash will help lessen the symptoms.

Also when going into ketosis you will probably feel less hungry. This is because the body is learning to use food more efficiently. This is also because carbs are digested quickly and leave you feeling hungry soon after eating them. And protein and fat take longer to digest, so you will feel less hungry than before.

The keto flu, like the flu that is brought on by a virus, can leave you feeling exhausted. Part of this is due to the decreased intake of carbs that give instant energy to the body. Part of this may be caused by slight dehydration.

Excess fat stored in the body holds water, which is why the first few pounds lost on any diet are water weight. You can combat this fatigue by drinking more water and by drinking sugar-free sports drinks with electrolytes.

And during the first few days of ketosis, you will likely see a decrease in your performance while exercising. While exercise is important to weight loss it might be necessary during this time to lessen the intensity of your workouts. Also, your muscles need time to become adjusted to the difference in the source of the fuel they are receiving.

Some people experience issues with the digestive system like diarrhea or constipation. Constipation is usually more of an issue that diarrhea is. Diarrhea comes from an increased intake of fat in the diet and your body will become used to the increase of fat in your diet. Constipation comes from not drinking enough water and from not eating enough vegetables. There are certain low carb veggies that are allowed on the keto diet and these should be eaten daily to keep your system regular.

Following a ketogenic plan should not be thought of as a diet plan but it should be viewed as a lifestyle change. This is a way of eating that can be done for many years. As long as you follow the keto diet you will continue to enjoy the benefits of the keto diet.

What is Ketogenic Diet?

Many people will shorten the ketogenic diet down and just call it a keto diet. This word was created because when you do this diet, your body will create small fuel molecules that are called ketones. These get used as an alternate source of fuel for our bodies. These get used when the body's glucose supplies get low.

When you don't eat a whole lot of carbs, these ketones are produced. This holds true when protein intake is kept at a moderate level. Eating too much protein can cause the body to turn it into sugar.

Your liver is able to create ketones from the fat your body has stored. The body then uses these ketones as fuel for many different parts of the body including the brain. Amazingly, the brain uses a lot of energy in just one day.

Low Carb

A keto diet is a very strict low carb diet. You are going to eat only 20 grams or less of net carbs each day.

When you have achieved your weight loss goals, you can begin to increase your carb intake. This needs to be done slowly so you don't gain the weight back.

Basics

This is a great diet, but there is a right and wrong way to do it. You have to begin this diet the right way so you will get faster and better results.

In theory, a keto diet is simple; low carbs, high fat. This isn't telling you what you can and can't eat. There is a list of complete foods you are allowed to eat, which we will discuss later. For now, here is a list of what you can eat:

- Heavy fats like tallow, olive oil, bacon fat, butter, lard, ghee, and coconut oil.

- Meats including organ meat.

- Eggs

- Fish and seafood

- Nonstarchy vegetables. All the leafy greens you want.

- Berries such as strawberries, blueberries, and raspberries.

Your typical day might look something like:

- Breakfast might include eggs and bacon.

- Lunch might be a chicken salad with a cup of bone broth.

- Dinner might be a steak with a side of veggies and a keto friendly dessert.

Some people like to snack between meals. If you are one of these people, some good choices are broth, cheese sticks, nuts, meat sticks, and celery sticks. You need to watch the number of snacks as these can make your total calorie count go up.

The keto diet is easy to personalize. You can experiment and find out what works best for you. Some people might realize they need more fat in their diet and others can eat fewer carbs. Some people even try intermittent fasting.

Many people who intermittent fast skip breakfast and will eat their first meat about one in the afternoon. This will up your ketosis power.

Macros

Macros have already been mentioned a few times. You are probably wondering by now what they are. Macros are short for macronutrients when used in the context of the keto diet.

Carbs are the only macro that you don't have to consume to stay alive. There are essential fatty and amino acids that are the building blocks of fats and proteins, but there aren't any essential carbs.

Carbs are made of two things: starch and sugar. Fiber is looked at as a carb, but with a keto diet, it isn't counted toward your total carb intake. Fiber isn't counted since the body doesn't digest fiber, so it doesn't have any effect on blood sugar.

When you look at a nutrition label, you need to first find the number of total carbs and then look for fiber. You are going to subtract the amount of fiber from the total number of carbs; this gives you the net carbs.

Total carbs – fiber = net carbs.

This just means that net carbohydrates only count the sugars and starches in the carbohydrates you eat.

In order for you to succeed, you need to find food that is naturally low in carbs and the ones that aren't. Not all foods are obvious. It is obvious that potatoes are high in carbs, but do you realize that bananas are also very high in carbs, too?

For anyone who is just beginning a keto diet, you need to try to consume about 20 grams of net carbs every day.

Protein is important for our bodies since it helps preserve lean muscle mass, the energy source in the absence of carbs makes hormones and enzymes, immune function, tissue repair, and growth. Protein plays an important role in biological processes. Proteins are the building blocks for healthy bodies.

When eaten, proteins are broken down into amino acids. Nine of these can't be produced by our bodies. This is why these essential amino acids need to come from foods. These nine include lysine, valine, threonine, histidine, isoleucine, tryptophan, leucine, phenylalanine, and methionine. If there is a deficiency in protein or any of these amino acids, it could cause malnutrition, kwashiorkor, or many other health problems.

When you are doing a keto diet, you have to be sure you are eating enough protein to preserve your lean body mass. The amount you consume, all depends on how much lean body mass you have now. Here is a guideline:

- .7 to .8 grams of protein per pound of muscle to help preserve your muscle mass.

- .8 to 1.2 grams of protein per pound of muscle to help you increase your muscle mass.

You don't want to lose any body mass, only gain or preserve it. Many people just focus on losing weight, but many times when people lose weight, they also lose muscle along with fat. Your goal needs to be losing weight while saving your muscle. This is important to keep up your metabolism.

The main thing is to make sure you don't get crazy when consuming protein when doing a keto diet. Too much might put too much stress on the kidneys and can affect ketosis. Try keeping your macros in the above ranges.

Here's an example:

Let's say you weigh 160 pounds and you have 30 percent body fat. This means you have about 48 pounds of body fat. Now you are going to subtract your body fat from your total weight and this gives you your lean body mass. For this, it would be 112 pounds.

In order to find the amount of protein you need to consume, you take the lean body mass number and multiply it by the ratio from earlier. In this example, you need to consume 89.6 grams of protein every day to preserve your muscle mass. It will look like this:

112 pounds muscle x .8 grams protein = 89.6 grams.

The last macro is fat. You need to consume the right amount of fat to maintain cell membranes, provide protective cushioning for organs, absorb certain vitamins, development, energy, and growth. These fats also help you feel fuller longer.

Dietary fat gets broken down into fatty acids and glycerol. The body can't synthesize two types of fatty acids, so it is important that you incorporate them into your diet. These fatty acids are linolenic acid and linoleic acid.

These facts are satiating, so it is perfect for people who want to fight off hunger pangs. You need to figure out how much fat you should eat. If your carbs are at a minimum, you have figured out how much protein you should eat, and then the rest of your dietary needs must be met with fat.

In order to maintain your weight, you are going to eat enough calories from fat in order to support your normal daily activities. If you want to burn fat, you need to eat in a deficit.

You have been given a lot of information to help you figure out your macros, but there are easier ways to figure this out. There are many online calculators that will figure these numbers without you getting a headache. If you would like to use an online calculator, check out this website: Ketogains. it works great.

If you would like to figure it out on your own, let's continue with the 160-pound example from above. Let's say this person is a female, stands 5'4", in her late 20s, and sits behind a desk all day. She is mainly sedentary.

Let's plug her into a calculator:

The base metabolic rate would be 1467 kcal.

Daily energy expenditure would be 1614 kcal.

She is going to need to consume about 90 grams of protein, 20 grams of net carbs, and 86 grams of fat. Her intake is 72 percent fat, 23 percent protein, and 5 percent carbs.

Now you know what macros are and how to find your numbers. You are on your way to beginning a ketogenic diet.

Advantage of the Vegetarian Ketogenic Diet

What Is A Vegetarian Ketogenic Diet?

A ketogenic diet is primarily a form of diet wherein the carb intake is restricted to ensure that the body enters a state of ketosis. The energy which is broken down is used for carrying out the different body activities.

In a normal diet in which carbs are regularly consumed, the body is in a state of glycolysis, a process by which carbohydrates are broken down into glucose molecules which are used as energy. However, when the body enters a state of ketosis, as discussed above, fat molecules are used as energy, helping to rid the body of excess fat ensuring weight loss.

Now, shifting our focus to the vegetarian ketogenic diet, the key difference here is that the recipes which we will share will all be vegetarian-based and won't include any kind of meat products whatsoever. The vegetarian ketogenic diet can be followed by both vegetarians and non-vegetarians. So, let us discuss some more details about the vegetarian ketogenic diet.

The Advantages of the Vegetarian Keto Diet Over Other Diets

When compared to most other diets, the vegetarian keto diet surely has many advantages to offer. Let us see the primary ones.

Systematic weight loss: This method of dieting leads to a systematic loss of weight. Do not expect to lose 10 kg in 10 days, but you will see your weight shedding systematically, and you are not likely to put it back again.

Muscular strength: Many forms of dieting are known to lead to loss of muscles as well. When you choose to opt for veg ketogenic diet, you will find that your muscular mass will be retained. You won't become lanky or feel lethargic because your muscles will still have the same kind of strength despite dieting.

You remain vegetarian: One of the best possible things about this diet is that for vegetarians, you do not have to alter your way of living. You still get your vegetarian options and still get to cut down your unwanted pounds without any trouble.

So, with these many possible advantages, it is definitely a recommended form of diet. Now that you have the incentives to opt for this diet form, let us explore more details.

The Aspects of Vegetarian Ketogenic Diet

Let us see some of the core aspects pertaining to this form of ketogenic diet.

The tips First off, a word to the wise: prepare yourself for the keto flu. Many begin the dieting regiment with a great deal of excitement and enthusiasm, but within a week or two, it is likely that some not-so-exciting symptoms will develop. You may feel lethargic, have a mild headache, suffer from nausea, and even lose your appetite for anything and everything. This is what is known as the keto flu, and it is a common reaction your body undergoes when switching from carbs to fat as a source of energy. Stay strong and beat the flu and once the symptoms subside, you will be all set to follow the diet regiment again.

Be mindful of what you are eating. The ketogenic diet mainly aims at cutting down carb intake, but this doesn't mean that you can binge on fat products. You need to be sensible about what you are eating and be logical in your dieting pattern.

Follow the diet regiment thoroughly. It can be a little hard at the beginning, but with time, you should be able to follow it. So, despite the inevitable craving for carbs and high-fat foods, you should try to stay strong and curb the appetite for it. The results will help you in the long run.

The Incentives

Reduces the chance of heart disease

To give you even more incentive for the vegetarian ketogenic diet, let us give you a snapshot of the numerous benefits which you can reap simply from following this dieting pattern.

The keto diet has the potential to reduce the chances of heart disease. While this diet is known to lower the level of bad cholesterol in the body, it also improves the level of good cholesterol. Similarly, the diet can also cut down the level of triglycerides. So, all these cumulative changes are known to help in reducing the chances of heart disease.

Stabilizes the body's metabolism

The keto diet is also known to stabilize the metabolism of the body. While you might experience some taxing side-effects initially, your body will quickly adapt, and it won't be long before you inevitably begin to notice the benefits. Over time, your appetite will be molded by the keto diet regiment, and your body will naturally enter a state of metabolic stability.

Improved energy

The ketogenic diet is also known to result in an increase in energy levels as well. It is very common for people to feel much more energetic and to experience a significant improvement in their ability to focus. So, those who would like to increase their attention span should definitely consider following a vegetarian keto diet.

The Mistakes to Avoid

Now, let us see some of the common mistakes which you should try to avoid.

Do not give up.

No matter how hard it feels initially, stay committed to following the diet. After a week, your body will adjust to the new pattern, and this will help you follow the diet in a much easier way. So, you need to be committed to following the diet.

Do not binge eat.

The ketogenic diet doesn't mean that you can consume as much food as you want as long as it's not carbs. You need to understand the calories you are consuming and be systematic in your diet intake. Avoid carbs and also avoid all kinds of junk food as well.

Stay strong during the keto flu.

Be prepared to be hit by the keto flu and stay strong because this will give you a great head start in following the ketogenic diet. So even when the body feels a little down, stick to your diet, and the flu symptoms are likely to subside in a week or two.

Take care of your health.

Along with the keto diet, you should be mindful of your health. Try and add at least some minor workouts to your routine, such as a short jog, and it should help you stay fit much more easily.

Use these pointers and the positive changes will be apparent.

The Nutrients

Whenever you follow a ketogenic diet, it is important to be mindful of the nutrients. This means you should have an accurate picture of what to eat and what to avoid.

The food to restrict in the ketogenic vegetarian diet

Let us now give you details regarding which food you should exclude from your diet when choosing the vegetarian keto style of eating.

•   All grains (even whole grain products) such as oats, barley, sorghum, and rice have to be avoided at all costs.

•   You should also avoid things like sugar, honey, maple syrup, and agave as well.

•   It's common knowledge that fruit is generally a healthy food choice, but following the keto vegetarian diet means that you need to steer clear of fruits like apple, oranges, and even bananas.

•   Lentils, peas, and even black beans should also be avoided.

•   Potatoes, yams, and related tubers are on the do-not-eat list as well.

The food to include in the keto vegetarian diet

Now, let us focus on the different foods you are allowed to eat while following this diet.

•   Leafy green vegetables, like spinach and kale, are a good choice.

- Vegetables that are grown above ground, like cauliflower, zucchini, and even broccoli, are good options.

- Tempeh, seitan tofu, and any high-protein, low-carb food products are a great addition to a meal.

- Try to include nuts and seeds in your diet. Pumpkin seeds, sunflower seeds, almonds, and pistachios are just a few flavorful options.

- If you're feeling adventurous, try to cook with sea vegetables, such as bladderwrack or kelp.

- Feel free to add fermented foods, like sauerkraut and kimchi, to your meals.

- Foods which have a low glycemic index, including avocado, blackberries, and raspberries, can serve as a nutritious and flavorful addition to your keto vegetarian diet.

So, these are some of the elementary details regarding the ketogenic diet. With these many details, you should now have a very clear picture pertaining to how this whole diet works.

Many people have been following the keto diet for decades now, and there is no mistake that the results are clear and easy to witness. They not only managed to get rid of the extra pounds, but at the same time, they have greatly improved their overall health.

One of the key things which you need to remember when following the veg ketogenic diet is to be the fact that you must follow a systematic and disciplined approach. Your inability to do so would surely hamper the benefits that you would otherwise reap from this diet.

While you have many of the details now, you must be wondering about the possible meals you can cook. We do know that following a strictly vegetarian diet cuts down on many options, and this is why we are going to give you precise recipes which you can follow when making your own meals. With these meals, you will be able to successfully follow the ketogenic diet and observe the changes in your body as well.

How to Get Started

In order to lose weight, you must aim and maintain a calorie deficit. This means burning more energy than you consume. A typical female will consume around 1700 calories daily when dieting, and for men this figure will be roughly 2200, though the ideal target of course differs according to an individual's height, weight, and activity level.

Consuming less than this would be irresponsible. The effects of consuming too few calories can wreak havoc on your body. When you suddenly start consuming much less than your body is used to, it can kick into "starvation mode" and start breaking down muscle instead of fat in an effort to ensure the body's needs are met. This muscle loss will also show up as weight loss on the scale, but it goes without saying that this is not the goal you are attempting to achieve. Avoid retaining your excess fat and lose muscle.

Below are some guidelines to help ensure you are not consuming too many calories for the keto-vegan diet:

Be sure to combat cravings by taking advantage of the satiating effects of protein.

Avoid making the mistake of snacking on too many nuts, seeds, and other fat-rich nibbles when trying to lose weight. These foods are very calorie-dense.

If you have not seen any clear weight loss results after 2-3 weeks, you should consider monitoring your calorie intake closely.

Enjoy the many non-starchy vegetables such as cauliflower, spinach, kale, broccoli, zucchini, and bell peppers, as well as fruits like avocados or berries. These contain many micronutrients in addition to being low in carbs.

Drink water throughout the day the hydrate the body and fill the stomach.

There are two ways you can get started with a keto vegan diet. The first way is by simply jumping right in and cutting out all carbohydrates from your diet. This method can be quite shocking as the transition is very steep. However, the practitioner usually sees results in a quicker time frame and is less likely to deal with sugar withdrawal symptoms for a long period of time.

The second way involves slowly implementing keto vegan practices. This involves slowly reducing your carbohydrate consumption by progressively eating low amounts of carbs every day. The second way is less jarring to beginner practitioners and allows for a learning curve that is not so steep. While it can be easier for newbie keto vegan practitioners to follow the second method, it takes longer to see noticeable results.

The method that you choose to start the keto vegan diet is entirely up to you and depends on your goals and lifestyle. You can start by practicing one method, and then the other to see what works best for you.

No matter how you get started here are a few tips that are useful:

Clear the non-keto vegan foods out of your cupboards and refrigerator and fill them up with keto-vegan friendly food so that you have an easier time sticking to this diet.

Keep things simple at the beginning. Simply up your fat and protein intake and ensure that you are consuming less than 50 grams of carbohydrates every day without worrying too much about the comparative proportions of each. Adjust to the diet then worry about these later.

Consult a licensed health care practitioner before you begin the keto vegan diet. Ensure that you do not have any preexisting medical conditions that might need addressing before you begin this diet.

Foods to Eat

Vegetables

Vegetables contain essential fiber, vitamins, minerals, and phytochemicals. Therefore, it has a high priority in a healthy diet and is vital for our digestive system.

Allowed vegetables:

Spinach, cucumber, broccoli, cauliflower, zucchini, Brussels sprouts, Chinese cabbage, fennel, kale, celeriac, radishes, asparagus, savoy cabbage, asparagus, avocado, bitter green, bok choi, cauliflower, cabbage, celery, chard, cabbage, endive, kohlrabi, lettuce, Nori, olives, radishes, summer squash, artichoke.

Recommendation: In a ketogenic diet, you should focus on low-starch vegetables. However, there is nothing wrong with eating sweet potato, pumpkin, or beetroot now and then.

Healthy fat

Healthy fat is the primary source of energy in a ketogenic diet. Approximately 70-80% of all calories should come from this category.

Allowed fat:

Coconut oil, olive oil, avocado oil, MCT oil, caprylic acid, krill oil, vegan butter, grape ghee, sunflower lecithin, almond paste, cocoa butter.

Recommendation: Consume at least two tablespoons of MCT oil or pure caprylic acid daily. The body converts the medium-chain fatty acids contained into three metabolic steps.

High-quality proteins

For a properly conducted ketogenic diet, one should not exaggerate the protein consumption.

Allowed foods:

Grape-based collagen hydrolysate, vegetable protein powder.

Recommendation: Do not overdo protein consumption. Instead, pay good attention to the quality of your protein source.

Fruits and berries

Although fruits contain vitamins and minerals, they often also contain large amounts of fructose. You can measure the effect on your ketosis.

Allowed:

Blueberries, strawberries, blackberries, raspberries, elderberries, currants, avocado, papaya.

Recommendation: Focus on low-sugar fruits such as berries. Treat her like some sweets. For example, you can make a delicious berry sorbet with frozen blueberries for dessert.

Drinks

Water, water with lemon juice, herbal tea, coffee, high-quality green tea, homemade lemonade, homemade ice tea, coconut milk, and almond milk (unsweetened).

Recommendation: It is essential to drink enough water. Try to take at least 2-3 liters of fluid daily.

Nuts and seeds

Macadamia, almond, coconut, pecans, walnuts, and cashews.

Recommendation: Since nuts are rich in trace elements, but also contain anti-nutrients such as phytic acid, you should limit the consumption to a handful per day.

Ketogenic alternatives

Keto Mayonnaise, Keto Biscuits, 85% Chocolate, Keto Cocoa, Keto Energy Balls, Keto Gummy Bears.

Recommendation: It is always practical to have delicious and ketogenic alternatives to the small sins of the diet at home. For example, in our office, we always have ketogenic mayonnaise and ketogenic biscuits.

Foods to Avoid

Of course, you should be careful to keep your consumption of carbohydrates low in a ketogenic diet. But by now, you have also learned that we are not only concerned with the macronutrients, but also the quality of the food to eat and the effect on your health.

Here you can find out which foods are not part of a healthy ketogenic diet.

Sugar in all forms

Sugar (sucrose), corn syrup (GFS, HFCS), agave syrup, molasses, brown sugar, granulated sugar, cane sugar, caramel, coconut sugar, palm sugar, sugarcane juice, fruit juice, fruit juice concentrate, sugar beet syrup, glucose, invert sugar, molasses.

Ketogenic alternative: xylitol, erythritol, stevia, ribose, primal sweet.

Artificial additives / food

Artificial flavors, artificial colors, artificial sugar substitutes, trans fat, bouillon.

Ketogenic alternative: real ingredients that provide real flavors!

Cereal products

Cereal products contain large amounts of fast carbohydrates and will immediately kick you out of ketosis. Therefore, you should avoid them. This includes:

Bread, pasta, cake, biscuits, pizza, cornmeal

Tip: You do not have to do without tasty pasta entirely if you know the right alternatives. For example, there is super delicious gluten-free bread or ketogenic spaghetti.

Alternatives: coconut flour, almond flour.

A Meal Plan for your First Month

Day	Breakfast	Lunch	Snack	Dinner	Dessert
1	Coconut Porridge with Blackberries	Delish Carrots	Nori Snack Rolls	Seitan Tex-Mex Casserole	Strawberry Coconut Parfait
2	Strawberry Chia Pudding	Glazed Carrots	Risotto Bites	Avocado Coconut Pie	Lemon-Chocolate Truffles
3	Raspberry Almond Smoothie	Sweet & Spicy Carrots	Jicama and Guacamole	Baked Mushrooms with Creamy Brussels Sprouts	Blackberry and Red Wine Crumble
4	Vanilla Yogurt Pancakes	Bell Pepper Gumbo	Curried Tofu "Egg Salad" Pitas	Pimiento Tofu balls	Cinnamon-Chocolate Cake
5	Broccoli Hash Browns	Italian Bell Pepper Platter	Garden Patch Sandwiches on Multigrain Bread	Tempeh with Garlic Asparagus	Himalayan Raspberry Fat Bombs
6	Sesame-Chia Bread	Green Goddess Buddha Bowl	Garden Salad Wraps	Mushroom Curry Pie	Cashew-Chocolate Cheesecake
7	No-Bread Avocado Sandwich	Cauliflower Rice and Mushroom Risotto	Black Sesame Wonton Chips	Spicy Cheese with Tofu Balls	Creamy Avocado Drink
8	Pear Oatmeal	Grilled Eggplant Roll-Ups	Marinated Mushroom Wraps	Tempeh Coconut Curry Bake	Raspberry Cookies
9	Pumpkin Oatmeal	Eggplant Gratin with Feta Cheese	Tamari Toasted Almonds	Kale and Mushroom Pierogis	Lenny & Larry's Cookies

10	Veggie Burrito	Tofu Pesto Zoodles	Avocado and Tempeh Bacon Wraps	Mushroom Lettuce Wraps	Zucchini Chocolate Brownies
11	Apple Steel Cut Oats	Cheesy Mushroom Pie	Kale Chips	Tofu and Spinach Lasagna with Red Sauce	Fudgy Pumpkin Brownies
12	Tofu Casserole	Meatless Florentine Pizza	Tempeh-Pimiento Cheese Ball	Green Avocado Carbonara	Cinnamon Roll Bars
13	Carrot Mix	Margherita Pizza with Cauliflower Crust	Seaweed Crackers	Cashew Buttered Quesadillas with Leafy Greens	Snickers Bars
14	Blueberries Oats	Almond Tofu Loaf	Sesame Tamari Almonds	Zucchini Boats with Vegan Cheese	Lemon Coconut Crack Bars
15	Apple and Pears Mix	Kale and Mushroom Biryani	Edamame Avocado Hummus	Tempeh Garam Masala Bake	Gingerbread Cookie Bars
16	Bell Pepper Oatmeal	Mushroom Pizza Bowls with Avocado & Cilantro	Pizza Cheese Ball	Caprese Casserole	Cocoa Berries Mousse
17	Banana and Walnuts Oats	Pistachios and Cheese Stuffed Zucchinis	Tahini Keto Bagels	Lemon Garlic Mushrooms	Nutmeg Pudding
18	Simple Granola	Soy Chorizo-Asparagus Bowl	Zucchini Nests	Almond Green Beans	Lime Cherries and Rice Pudding
19	Zucchini Oatmeal	Creamy Brussels Sprouts Bowls	Low Carb Bibimbap	Fried Okra	Chocolate Pudding
20	Cranberry Coconut Quinoa	Green Beans and Radishes Bake	Walnut Carrot Bombs	Super Healthy Beet Greens Salad	Coffee and Rhubarb Cream

21	Gingerbread Porridge	Avocado and Radish Bowls	Nutty Zucchini Salad	Coconut Yogurt with Chia Seeds and Almonds	Chocolate Sea Salt Almonds
22	Overnight Strawberry Cheesecake Porridge	Celery and Radish Soup	Kale Pate Spread	Super Delicious Cucumber Salad	Salted Caramel Cashew Brittle
23	Blueberry Quinoa Porridge	Lime Avocado and Cucumber Soup	Smoked Almonds	Pudding Delight with Banana & Coconut	Cookies and Cream Parfait
24	Blueberry Chia Pudding	Avocado and Kale Soup	Roasted Garlic Mushrooms	Extra Easy Cheese Sandwich	Pecan Pie Pudding
25	Almond Flour Muffins	Spinach and Cucumber Salad	Mediterranean Cucumber Bites	India Super Easy Summer Cooler	Chocolate Avocado Pudding
26	Coconut Porridge with Blackberries	Delish Carrots	Nori Snack Rolls	Seitan Tex-Mex Casserole	Strawberry Coconut Parfait
27	Strawberry Chia Pudding	Glazed Carrots	Risotto Bites	Avocado Coconut Pie	Lemon-Chocolate Truffles
28	Raspberry Almond Smoothie	Sweet & Spicy Carrots	Jicama and Guacamole	Baked Mushrooms with Creamy Brussels Sprouts	Blackberry and Red Wine Crumble
29	Vanilla Yogurt Pancakes	Bell Pepper Gumbo	Curried Tofu "Egg Salad" Pitas	Pimiento Tofu balls	Cinnamon-Chocolate Cake
30	Broccoli Hash Browns	Italian Bell Pepper Platter	Garden Patch Sandwiches on Multigrain Bread	Tempeh with Garlic Asparagus	Himalayan Raspberry Fat Bombs

Breakfast Recipes

1. Coconut Porridge with Blackberries

Preparation Time: 7 Minutes

Cooking Time: 5 Minutes

Servings: 4

Ingredients:

For the flax egg:

1 tbsp flax seed powder + 3 tbsp water

1 tbsp olive oil

1 tbsp coconut flour

1 pinch ground chia seeds

5 tbsp coconut cream

1 pinch salt

Thawed frozen blackberries to serve

Directions:

In a small bowl, mix the flax seed powder with the water and allow thickening for 5 minutes.

Place a non-stick saucepan over low heat and mix all the ingredients except for the blackberries. Cook the mixture while stirring continuously until your desired thickness is achieved.

Turn the heat off and spoon the porridge into serving bowls.

Top with some blackberries and serve immediately.

Nutrition:

Calories:131 Cal Fat:13.3 g

Carbs: 3 g Fiber: 1g Protein:2 g

2. Strawberry Chia Pudding

Preparation Time: 10 Minutes

Cooking Time: 0

Servings: 4

Ingredients:

1 ½ cups coconut milk

½ cup dairy-free plain yogurt

4 tsp sugar-free maple syrup

1 tsp vanilla extract

7 tbsp chia seeds

1 cup fresh strawberries + extra for garnishing

Chopped almonds to garnish

Mint leaves to garnish

Directions:

In a bowl, mix all the ingredients up to the chia seeds.

Mash the strawberries in a bowl using a fork and stir the puree into the yogurt mixture.

Divide the mix into four medium mason jars, cover the lids and refrigerate for 30 minutes to thicken the pudding.

Take out the jars, remove the lids, and stir the pudding. Garnish with two strawberries each, almonds, and some mint leaves.

Serve immediately.

Nutrition:

Calories: 240 Cal

Fat:22.6 g

Carbs: 9 g

 Fiber: 3 g

Pro tein: 3 g

3. Raspberry Almond Smoothie

Preparation Time: 2 Minutes

Cooking Time: 0

Servings: 4

Ingredients:

1 ½ cups almond milk or coconut milk

3 tbsp coconut cream

½ cup raspberries

Juice from half lemon

½ tsp almond extract

Directions:

Process all the ingredients in a high-speed blender until smooth.

Pour into serving cups and enjoy.

Nutrition:

Calories:216 Cal

Fat:21.7 g

Carbs: 7 g

Fiber: 3g

Protein:3 g

4. Vanilla Yogurt Pancakes

Preparation Time: 8 Minutes

Cooking Time: 15 Minutes

Servings: 4

Ingredients:

½ cup almond flour

½ tsp baking powder

1 tbsp erythritol

½ cup dairy-free plain yogurt

1 lemon, juiced

1 vanilla pod, caviar extracted

2 tbsp unsalted vegan butter

2 tbsp olive oil

Sugar-free maple syrup to serve

Dairy-free plain yogurt to serve

Choice of berries to serve

Directions:

Sift the almo nd flour and baking powder into a medium bowl and mix in the erythritol.

In a small bowl, whisk the yogurt, lemon juice. Combine both mixtures, add the vanilla caviar and whisk well until smooth.

In a medium skillet set over medium heat, melt a quarter each of the vegan butter and olive oil. Add 1 ½ tablespoons of the pancake mixture into the pan and cook for 3 to 4 minutes or until small bubbles begin to show.

Flip the pancake and cook the other side until set and golden, 2 minutes. Repeat cooking until the batter finishes using the remaining vegan butter and olive oil in the same proportions.

Plate the pancakes, drizzle with some maple syrup, top with a generous dollop of yogurt, and scatter some berries on top.

Serve immediately.

Nutrition:

Calories:165 Cal

Fat: 14.9g

Carbs: 3 g,

Fiber:0 g

Protein:6 g

5. Broccoli Hash Browns

Preparation Time: 10 Minutes

Cooking Time: 24 Minutes

Servings: 4

Ingredients:

3 tbsp flax seed powder + 9 tbsp water

1 big head broccoli, riced

½ white onion, grated

1 tsp salt

1 tbsp black pepper

5 tbsp vegan butter, for frying

Directions:

In a medium bowl, mix the flax seed powder with the water and allow thickening for 5 minutes.

Mix in the broccoli, onion, salt, and black pepper. Allow sitting for 5 minutes to thicken the mixture.

Place a large non-stick skillet over medium heat and melt in 1/3 of the vegan butter.

Ladle scoops of the broccoli mixture into the skillet (about 3 to 4 hash browns per batch), flatten the pancakes to measure 3 to 4 inches in diameter and fry until golden brown on one side, 4 minutes.

Turn the pancakes and cook the other side until brown too, 5 minutes.

Plate the pancakes, make more, and serve warm.

Nutrition:

Calories: 216 Cal Fat:21.3 g

Carbs:5 g Fiber:2 g, Protein:4 g

6. Sesame-Chia Bread

Preparation Time: 10minutes

Cooking Time: 45minutes

Servings: 6

Ingredients:

3 tbsp ground flax seeds

½ cup + 1 tbsp water

2/3 cup cream cheese, room temperature

¼ cup melted coconut oil

2 tbsp sesame oil

¾ cup coconut cream

¾ cup coconut flour

1 cup almond flour

3 tsp baking powder

5 1/3 tbsp sesame seeds

½ cup chia seeds

¼ cup psyllium husk powder

1 tsp salt   1 tbsp poppy seeds

Directions:

Preheat the oven to 350 F and line a 4 x 7-inch loaf pan with baking paper.

In a medium bowl, whisk the flax seed powder with the water, and allow soaking for 5 minutes.

Using an electric hand mixer, whisk in the cream cheese, coconut oil, sesame oil, and coconut cream.

In another bowl, mix the coconut flour, almond flour, baking powder, sesame seeds, chia seeds, psyllium husk powder, and salt.

Blend both mixtures until dough forms.

Transfer the dough to the loaf pan, sprinkle with the poppy seeds, and bake in the oven for 45 minutes or until a skewer inserted into the bread comes out clean.

Remove the parchment paper with the bread and allow cooling on a rack.

Slice and serve the bread for breakfast.

Nutrition: Calories: 570 Fat: 57.6g

Carbs: 12 g Fiber:5 g Protein:10 g

7. No-Bread Avocado Sandwich

Preparation Time: 10 Minutes

Cooking Time: 0

Servings: 2

Ingredients:

2 oz. little gem lettuce, 2 leaves extracted

½ oz vegan butter

1 oz sliced vegan cheese

1 avocado, pitted, peeled, and sliced

1 large red tomato, sliced

Chopped fresh parsley to garnish

Directions:

Rinse and pat dry the lettuce leave. Arrange on a flat plate (with inner side facing you) to serve as the base of the sandwich.

Spread some butter on each leaf, top with the cheese, avocado, and tomato.

Garnish with some parsley and serve the sandwich immediately.

Nutrition:

Calories:143 Cal

Fat: 12.7g

Carbs:6 g

Fiber: 4 g

Protein: 4g

8. Pear Oatmeal

Preparation Time: 10 Minutes

Cooking Time: 15 Minutes

Servings: 3

Ingredients:

2 cups coconut milk

½ cup steel cut oats

½ teaspoon vanilla extract

1 pear, chopped

½ teaspoon maple extract

1 tablespoon stevia

Directions:

In your air fryer's pan, mix coconut milk with oats, vanilla, pear, maple extract and stevia, stir, cover and cook at 360 degrees F for 15 minutes.

Divide into bowls and serve for breakfast.

Enjoy!

Nutrition:

Calories: 200 Cal

Fat: 5 g

Fiber: 7 g

Carbs 14 g

Protein: 4 g

9. Pumpkin Oatmeal

Preparation Time: 10 Minutes

Cooking Time: 20 Minutes

Servings: 4

Ingredients:

1 and ½ cups water

½ cup pumpkin puree

1 teaspoon pumpkin pie spice

3 tablespoons stevia

½ cup steel cut oats

Directions:

In your air fryer's pan, mix water with oats, pumpkin puree, pumpkin spice and stevia, stir, cover and cook at 360 degrees F for 20 minutes

Divide into bowls and serve for breakfast.

Enjoy!

Nutrition:

Calories: 21 Cal

Fat: $ g

Fiber: 7 g

Carbs 8 g

Protein: 3 g

10. Veggie Burrito

Preparation Time: 10 Minutes

Cooking Time: 15 Minutes

Servings: 8

Ingredients:

16 ounces tofu, crumbled

1 green bell pepper, chopped

¼ cup scallions, chopped

15 ounces canned black beans, drained

1 cup vegan salsa

½ cup water

¼ teaspoon cumin, ground

½ teaspoon turmeric powder

½ teaspoon smoked paprika

A pinch of salt and black pepper

¼ teaspoon chili powder

3 cups spinach leaves, torn

8 vegan tortillas for serving

Directions:

In your air fryer, mix tofu with bell pepper, scallions, black beans, salsa, water, cumin, turmeric, paprika, salt, pepper and chili powder, stir, cover and cook at 370 degrees F for 20 minutes

Add spinach, toss well, divide this on your vegan tortillas, roll, wrap them and serve for breakfast.

Enjoy!

Nutrition:

Calories: 211 Cal

Fat: 4 g

Fiber: 7 g

Carbs 14 g

Protein: 4 g

11. Apple Steel Cut Oats

Preparation Time: 10 Minutes

Cooking Time: 15 Minutes

Servings: 6

Ingredients:

1 and ½ cups water

1 and ½ cups coconut milk

2 apples, cored, peeled and chopped

1 cup steel cut oats

½ teaspoon cinnamon powder

¼ teaspoon nutmeg, ground

¼ teaspoon allspice, ground

¼ teaspoon ginger powder

¼ teaspoon cardamom, ground

1 tablespoon flaxseed, ground

2 teaspoons vanilla extract

2 teaspoons stevia

Cooking spray

Directions:

Spray your air fryer with cooking spray, add apples, milk, water, cinnamon, oats, allspice, nutmeg, cardamom, ginger, vanilla, flaxseeds and stevia, stir, cover and cook at 360 degrees F for 15 minutes

Divide into bowls and serve for breakfast.

Enjoy!

Nutrition:

Calories: 172 Cal

Fat: 3 g

Fiber: 7 g

Carbs 8 g

Protein: 5 g

12. Tofu Casserole

Preparation Time: 10 Minutes

Cooking Time: 20 Minutes

Servings: 4

Ingredients:

1 teaspoon lemon zest, grated

14 ounces tofu, cubed

1 tablespoon lemon juice

2 tablespoons nutritional yeast

1 tablespoon apple cider vinegar

1 tablespoon olive oil

2 garlic cloves, minced

10 ounces spinach, torn

½ cup yellow onion, chopped

½ teaspoon basil, dried

8 ounces mushrooms, sliced

Salt and black pepper to the taste

¼ teaspoon red pepper flakes

Cooking spray

Directions:

Spray your air fryer with some cooking spray, arrange tofu cubes on the bottom, add lemon zest, lemon juice, yeast, vinegar, olive oil, garlic, spinach, onion, basil, mushrooms, salt, pepper and pepper flakes, toss, cover and cook at 365 degrees F for 20 minutes.

Divide between plates and serve for breakfast.

Enjoy!

Nutrition Value: calories 246, fat 6, fiber 8, carbs 12, protein 4

Nutrition: Calories: 2460 Cal

Fat: 6 g Fiber: 8 g Carbs 12 g Protein: 4 g

13. Carrot Mix

Preparation Time: 10 Minutes

Cooking Time: 15 Minutes

Servings: 4

Ingredients:

2 cups coconut milk

½ cup steel cut oats

1 cup carrots, shredded

1 teaspoon cardamom, ground

½ teaspoon agave nectar

A pinch of saffron

Cooking spray

Directions:

Spray your air fryer with cooking spray, add milk, oats, carrots, cardamom and agave nectar, stir, cover and cook at 365 degrees F for 15 minutes

Divide into bowls, sprinkle saffron on top and serve for breakfast.

Enjoy!

Nutrition Value: calories 202, fat 7, fiber 4, carbs 8, protein 3

Nutrition:

Calories: 202 Cal Fat: 7 g

Fiber: 4 g Carbs 8 g

Protein: 8 g

14. Blueberries Oats

Preparation Time: 10 Minutes

Cooking Time: 15 Minutes

Servings: 4

Ingredients:

1 cup blueberries

1 cup steel cut oats

1 cup coconut milk

2 tablespoons agave nectar

½ teaspoon vanilla extract

Cooking spray

Directions:

Spray your air fryer with cooking spray, add oats, milk, agave nectar, vanilla and blueberries, toss, cover and cook at 365 degrees F for 10 minutes.

Divide into bowls and serve for breakfast.

Enjoy!

Nutrition:

Calories: 202 Cal

Fat: 6 g

Fiber: 8 g

Carbs 9g

Protein: 6 g

15. Apple and Pears Mix

Preparation Time: 10 Minutes

Cooking Time: 15 Minutes

Servings: 6

Ingredients:

4 apples, cored, peeled and cut into medium chunks

1 teaspoon lemon juice

4 pears, cored, peeled and cut into medium chunks

5 teaspoons stevia

1 teaspoon cinnamon powder

1 teaspoon vanilla extract

½ teaspoon ginger, ground

½ teaspoon cloves, ground

½ teaspoon cardamom, ground

Directions:

In your air fryer, mix apples with pears, lemon juice, stevia, cinnamon, vanilla extract, ginger, cloves and cardamom, stir, cover, cook at 360 degrees F for 15 minutes

Divide into bowls and serve for breakfast.

Enjoy!

Nutrition:

Calories:161 Cal

Fat: 3 g Fiber: 7 g Carbs 9 g Protein: 4 g

16. Bell Pepper Oatmeal

Preparation Time: 10 Minutes

Cooking Time: 15 Minutes

Servings: 2

Ingredients:

1 cup steel cut oats

2 tablespoons canned kidney beans, drained

2 red bell peppers, chopped

4 tablespoons coconut cream

A pinch of sweet paprika

Salt and black pepper to the taste

¼ teaspoon cumin, ground

Directions:

Heat up your air fryer at 360 degrees F, add oats, beans, bell peppers, coconut cream, paprika, salt, pepper and cumin, stir, cover and cook for 16 minutes.

Divide into bowls and serve for breakfast.

Enjoy!

Nutrition:

Calories: 173Cal

Fat: 4 g Fiber: 6 g

Carbs 12 g Protein: 4 g

17. Banana and Walnuts Oats

Preparation Time: 10 Minutes

Cooking Time: 15 Minutes

Servings: 4

Ingredients:

1 banana, peeled and mashed

1 cup steel cut oats

2 cups almond milk

2 cups water

¼ cup walnuts, chopped

2 tablespoons flaxseed meal

2 teaspoons cinnamon powder

1 teaspoon vanilla extract

½ teaspoon nutmeg, ground

Directions:

In your air fryer mix oats with almond milk, water, walnuts, flaxseed meal, cinnamon, vanilla and nutmeg, stir, cover and cook at 360 degrees F for 15 minutes.

Divide into bowls and serve for breakfast.

Enjoy!

Nutrition:

Calories: 181 Cal

Fat: 7 g Fiber: 6 g Carbs 12 g

Protein: 11 g

18. Simple Granola

Preparation Time: 10 Minutes

Cooking Time: 15 Minutes

Servings: 3

Ingredients:

½ cup granola

½ cup bran flakes

2 green apples, cored, peeled and roughly chopped

¼ cup apple juice

1/8 cup maple syrup

2 tablespoons cashew butter

1 teaspoon cinnamon powder

½ teaspoon nutmeg, ground

Directions:

In your air fryer, mix granola with bran flakes, apples, apple juice, maple syrup, cashew butter, cinnamon and nutmeg, toss, cover and cook at 365 degrees F for 15 minutes

Divide into bowls and serve for breakfast.

Enjoy!

Nutrition:

Calories: 188 Cal

Fat: 6 g Fiber: 9 g

Carbs 11 g Protein: 6 g

19. Zucchini Oatmeal

Preparation Time: 10 Minutes

Cooking Time: 15 Minutes

Servings: 4

Ingredients:

½ cup steel cut oats

1 carrot, grated

1 and ½ cups almond milk

¼ zucchini, grated

¼ teaspoon nutmeg, ground

¼ teaspoon cloves, ground

½ teaspoon cinnamon powder

2 tablespoons maple syrup

¼ cup pecans, chopped

1 teaspoon vanilla extract

Directions:

In your air fryer, mix oats with carrot, zucchini, almond milk, cloves, nutmeg, cinnamon, maple syrup, pecans and vanilla extract, stir, cover and cook at 365 degrees F for 15 minutes.

Divide into bowls and serve.

Enjoy!

Nutrition:

Calories: 175 Cal Fat: 4 g

Fiber: 7 g Carbs 12 g Protein: 7 g

20. Cranberry Coconut Quinoa

Preparation Time: 10 Minutes

Cooking Time: 13 Minutes

Servings: 4

Ingredients:

1 cup quinoa

3 cups coconut water

1 teaspoon vanilla extract

3 teaspoons stevia

1/8 cup coconut flakes

¼ cup cranberries, dried

1/8 cup almonds, chopped

Directions:

In your air fryer, mix quinoa with coconut water, vanilla, stevia, coconut flakes, almonds and cranberries, toss, cover and cook at 365 degrees F for 13 minutes.

Divide into bowls and serve for breakfast.

Enjoy!

Nutrition:

Calories: 146 Cal

Fat: 5 g

Fiber: 5 g

Carbs 10 g Protein: 7 g

21. Gingerbread Porridge

Preparation Time: 9 Minutes

Cooking Time: 2 Minutes

Servings: 2

Ingredients:

1/3 c. coconut milk, full-fat, canned

½ c. water

1 tbsp. coconut flour

¼ c. hemp seeds

½ c. flacked unsweetened coconut

1 ½ t. ground ginger

1 t. of the following:

ground cloves

ground nutmeg

vanilla

½ tbsp. ground cinnamon

1-2 teaspoons sweetener of your choice

Optional Toppings

Almond butter, chopped walnuts/pecans, cranberries

Directions:

In a medium saucepan, add the milk, water, coconut, coconut flour, & hemp seed.

Bring these ingredients to a boil, allowing to simmer 2 minutes or until thickened.

Add cinnamon, vanilla ginger, cloves, nutmeg, and combine until well-mixed and put in a heat-resistant bowl.

Sprinkle sweetener and any optional toppings of your choice across the top.

Mix and enjoy with additional milk as needed.

Nutrition:

Calories: 374 Cal

Proteins: 11 g

Carbos: 9 g

Fats: 33 g

22. Overnight Strawberry Cheesecake Porridge

Preparation Time: 10 Minutes

Cooking Time: 0

Servings: 1

Ingredients

¼ c. fresh strawberries

½ c. coconut milk

2 tbsp. of the following:

coconut yogurt

ground flaxseed

chia seeds

sweetener of your choice

1 tbsp. of the following:

almond flour

shredded unsweetened coconut

Directions:

Mix almond flour, unsweetened coconut, sweetener, chia seed, and flaxseed in a shallow bowl.

Next, pour ¼ cup of the coconut milk with dry contents and combine well.

Refrigerate overnight.

Before serving, add the remaining milk until the mixture becomes thick and creamy.

Layer the yogurt and strawberries on top.

Mix and enjoy.

Nutrition:

Calories: 275 Cal

Proteins: 8 g

Carbs: 16 g

Fats: 17 g

23. Blueberry Quinoa Porridge

Preparation Time: 20 Minutes

Cooking Time: 15 Minutes

Servings: 2

Ingredients:

1 c. blueberries

1/8 t. cinnamon

¼ t. vanilla

1 tbsp. sweetener of your choice

2 c. almond milk

1 c. uncooked quinoa

Optional Toppings

Chia seeds, hemp seeds, hazelnuts

Directions:

In a saucepan, add milk and quinoa.

Heat milk and quinoa at low heat for roughly 10 minutes, stirring to prevent scorching.

Slowly combine vanilla, cinnamon, and sugar and cook for 5 minutes or when the quinoa soft.

Take away from the heat and place in serving bowls.

Top with blueberries and sprinkle sweetener of your choice across the top.

Mix and enjoy.

Nutrition:

Calories: 374 Cal

Proteins: 11 g

Carbs: 9 g

Fats: 33 g

24. Blueberry Chia Pudding

Preparation Time: 8 Hours 10 Minutes

Cooking Time: 0

Servings: 3

Ingredients

1/8 t. cinnamon

½ t. vanilla

2 c. almond milk, unsweetened

1 tbsp. maple syrup

1/3 c. blueberries

6 tbsp. chia seeds, fresh

Directions:

Combine the chia seeds, blueberries, syrup, milk, vanilla, and cinnamon into a blender, blending into a silky consistency.

Separate mixture into 3 glasses or ramekins.

Chill overnight or until set, approximately 8 hours.

Enjoy it chilled.

Nutrition:

Calories: 374

Proteins: 11 g

Cars: 9 g

Fats: 33 g

25. Almond Flour Muffins

Preparation Time: 10 Minutes

Cooking Time: 15 Minutes

Servings: 4

Ingredients

¼ t. salt

½ tbsp. baking powder

1 flax egg

¼ c. almond milk

1 tbsp. stevia (or your sweetener of choice)

1 c. almond flour

Olive oil for greasing muffin pan.

Optional add-in

Crushed, walnuts, blueberries, sugar-free chocolate chips

Directions:

Set the oven to preheat at 35

Grease the muffin pan with olive oil.

Combine baking powder, stevia, salt, and almond flour in a mixing bowl. Mix completely.

Slowly add the flax egg and almond milk and mix well

If adding any add-ins, add them at this point (crushed walnuts, blueberries, chocolate chips).

Using a ¼ c. measuring cup, fill each muffin tin approximately 2/3 full.

Carefully slide into the oven and cook for 10 minutes (mini size) or 15 minutes (regular size).

Take it from oven and place in a cool area to allow muffins to cool while still in the tin for about 10 minutes. Then, carefully remove the muffins using a knife to loosen them from the sides of the tin.

Nutrition:

Calories: 217 Cal

Proteins: 11 g

Carbs: 9 g

Fats: 33 g

Lunch Recipes

26. Delish Carrots

Preparation Time: 15 Minutes

Cooking Time: 20 Minutes

Servings: 16

Ingredients:

2 tbsp. olive oil

1 chopped yellow onion

3 finely chopped garlic cloves

5 pounds halved medium baby carrots baby

½ cup homemade vegetable broth

1 tsp Italian seasoning

1 tsp spike seasoning

Directions:

Place the oil in the Instant Pot and select "Sauté". Then add the onion and garlic and cook for about 4-5 minutes.

Add the carrots and cook for about 4-5 minutes.

Select the "Cancel" and stir in collard greens and water.

Secure the lid and place the pressure valve to "Seal" position.

Select "Manual" and cook under "High Pressure" for about 10 minutes.

Select the "Cancel" and carefully do a "Natural" release for about 10 minutes and then do a "Quick" release.

Remove the lid and serve.

Nutrition:

Calories: 70 Cal Fat: 2.1g

Carbs: 0.78g Protein: 1.2g Fiber: 4.3g

27. Glazed Carrots

Preparation Time: 15 Minutes

Cooking Time: 4 Minutes

Servings: 8

Ingredients: 2 pounds baby carrots

1/3 cup butter 2 tbsp. Erythritol

1/2 tsp ground cinnamon

salt, to taste ½ cup water

Directions:

In the pot of Instant Pot, add all ingredients and stir to combine.

Secure the lid and place the pressure valve to "Seal" position.

Select "Manual" and cook under "High Pressure" for about 4 minutes.

Select the "Cancel" and carefully do a "Natural" release.

Remove the lid and serve.

Nutrition:

Calories: 91 Fat: 5.9g Carbs: 1.56g

Protein: 0.8g Fiber: 3.4g

28. Sweet & Spicy Carrots

Preparation Time: 18 Minutes

Cooking Time: 2 Minutes

Servings: 4

Ingredients:

1 pound quartered lengthwise and halved carrots

1 tbsp. Erythritol

2 tbsp. butter

3 tsp ground mustard

1 tsp ground cumin

½ tsp cayenne pepper

¼ tsp red pepper flakes

Salt and freshly ground black pepper, to taste

1/8 tsp ground cinnamon

Directions:

In the bottom of Instant Pot, arrange a steamer basket and pour 1 cup of water.

Place the carrots into the steamer basket.

Secure the lid and place the pressure valve to "Seal" position.

Select "Manual" and cook under "High Pressure" for about 1 minute.

Select the "Cancel" and carefully do a "Quick" release.

Remove the lid and transfer the carrots to a bowl.

Remove water from the pot and with paper towels, pat dry.

Select the "Sauté" mode for Power Pressure Cooker. In the pot of Pressure Cooker, melt butter and stir in the remaining ingredients.

Stir in the carrots and cook for about 1 minute.

Select the "Cancel" and serve warm with the sprinkling of cinnamon.

Nutrition:

Calories: 112

Fat: 6.6g Carbs: 3.50g Protein: 1.7g

Fiber: 3.3g

29. Bell Pepper Gumbo

Preparation Time: 20 Minutes

Cooking Time: 5 Minutes

Servings: 3

Ingredients:

tbsp. olive oil

4 minced garlic cloves

½ tsp cumin seeds

1 seeded and cut into long strips green bell pepper

1 seeded and cut into long strips red bell pepper

1 seeded and cut into long strips yellow bell pepper

1 seeded and cut into long strips bell pepper

½ tsp red chili powder

¼ tsp ground turmeric

Salt and freshly ground black pepper, to taste

¼ cup water

½ tbsp. fresh lemon juice

Directions:

Place the oil in the Instant Pot and select "Sauté". Then add the garlic and cumin and cook for about 1 minute.

Select the "Cancel" and stir in remaining ingredients except for lemon juice.

Secure the lid and place the pressure valve to "Seal" position.

Select "Manual" and cook under "High Pressure" for about 2 minutes.

Select the "Cancel" and carefully do a "Quick" release.

Remove the lid and select "Sauté".

Stir in lemon juice and cook for about 1-2 minutes.

Select the "Cancel" and serve.

Nutrition:

Calories 101 Total Fat 5.3g

Net Carbs 4.6g Protein 2g Fiber 2.5g

30. Italian Bell Pepper Platter

Preparation Time: 20 Minutes

Cooking Time: 10 Minutes

Servings: 5

Ingredients: tbsp. olive oil

1 cut into thin strips yellow onion

5 seeded and cut into long strips green bell peppers

very finely chopped medium ripe tomatoes

chopped garlic cloves

tbsp. fresh parsley

Salt and freshly ground black pepper, to taste

Directions:

Place the oil in the Instant Pot and select "Sauté". Then add the onion and cook for about 3-4 minutes.

Add the bell peppers and garlic clove and cook for about 5 minutes.

Select the "Cancel" and stir in remaining ingredients.

Secure the lid and place the pressure valve to "Seal" position.

Select "Manual" and cook under "High Pressure" for about 5-6 minutes.

Select the "Cancel" and carefully do a "Quick" release.

Remove the lid and serve.

Nutrition:

Calories 82 Total Fat 3.2g

Net Carbs 2.7g Protein 12.4g Fiber 2.7g

31. Green Goddess Buddha Bowl

Preparation Time: 10 Minutes

Cooking Time: 5 Minutes

Servings: 1

Ingredients:

2 cups fresh spinach

2 tablespoons avocado oil

4 broccolini spears

⅛ teaspoon salt

⅛ teaspoon freshly ground black pepper

⅓ cup frozen cauliflower rice, thawed

2 tablespoons shredded carrots

½ avocado, sliced

1 tablespoon almond butter, melted

1 tablespoon minced fresh cilantro

Directions:

Place the spinach in the bottom of a medium serving bowl.

In a skillet over medium-high heat, heat the avocado oil. Add the broccolini and sauté for 2 to 3 minutes. Season with the salt and pepper and transfer it to the bowl containing the spinach.

Add the cauliflower rice to the skillet and cook for 3 minutes. Add it to the serving bowl.

Top with the carrots and avocado.

Drizzle with the melted almond butter, sprinkle the cilantro on top, and serve.

Nutrition:

Calories 82 Total Fat 3.2g

Net Carbs 2.7g Protein 12.4g

Fiber 2.7g

32. Cauliflower Rice and Mushroom Risotto

Preparation Time: 20 Minutes

Cooking Time: 30 Minutes

Serving: 6

Ingredients:

Black pepper, one teaspoon

Salt, .5 teaspoon

Parsley, fresh, chopped, two tablespoons

Parmesan cheese, grated, .5 cup

Heavy cream, one cup

Cauliflower, riced, four cups

Vegetable broth, two cups divided

Mushrooms, button, one cup sliced thin

Shallot, one large, minced

Onion, one small, well diced

Garlic, minced, six cloves

Olive oil, two tablespoons

Butter, two tablespoons

Directions:

Add the olive oil and the butter together in one pan and fry the shallot, onion, and garlic for five minutes.

Pour in one cup of the vegetables broth and the mushrooms and cook for five more minutes.

To this mix and the other cup of vegetable broth and the riced cauliflower, cooking for ten minutes while stirring often.

Pour in the heavy cream, salt, pepper, parsley, and the parmesan cheese and turn the heat under the pot to low. Simmer this for ten to fifteen minutes or until the mix is thickened.

Nutrition: Calories 297 Cal

Carbs: 7.5 g Protein:7 Fat: 26 g

33. Grilled Eggplant Roll-Ups

Preparation Time: 5 Minutes

Cooking Time: 8 Minutes

Servings: 8

Ingredients:

Olive oil, two tablespoons

Basil, fresh, chopped, two tablespoons

Tomato, one large

Mozzarella cheese, four ounces

Eggplant, one medium

Directions:

After cutting off both of the ends of the eggplant slice it into strips the long way about a quarter inch thick. Slice the tomato and the mozzarella very thinly and set to the side.

Brush the olive oil onto the slices of eggplant and grill them in a skillet for three minutes on each side.

When both sides are grilled lay a slice of cheese and a slice of tomato on each zucchini slice. Sprinkle all with the black pepper and the basil, then let grill for two to three minutes until the cheese begins to soften.

Remove the slices from the skillet and lie on a plate, then carefully roll each slice as far as it will roll.

Nutrition:

Calorie 59 Carbs: 4 g

Protein: 3 g Fat: 3 g

34. Eggplant Gratin with Feta Cheese

Preparation Time: 15 Minutes

Cooking Time: 40 Minutes

Servings: 6

Ingredients: Salt, .5 teaspoon

Black pepper, .5 teaspoon

Olive oil, three tablespoons

Tomato sauce, .5 cup

Gruyere cheese, .75 cup,

Basil, fresh chop, .25 cup

Chives, chopped, one tablespoon

Thyme, chopped, one teaspoon

Feta cheese, crumbled, three ounces

Heavy cream, one cup

Eggplant, two, half-inch slices

Directions:

Heat oven to 375. Lay the eggplant slices on a baking pan and coat with olive oil and sprinkle on pepper and salt and bake the slices for twenty minutes.

While they are baking put the Feta cheese and heavy cream in a pot and let boil.

Remove the cooking pot from the heat and stir in the chives and thyme and set to the side.

Spread all of the tomato sauce on the bottom of a nine by thirteen baking pan and lay the eggplant slices over the bottom.

Cover the slices with the Gruyere cheese and the basil. Add another layer with the rest of the eggplant and cover all with the heavy cream mixture. Bake for twenty minutes.

Nutrition:

Calories: 302 Cal Carbs 14 g Protein: 9 g

Fat: 24 g

35. Tofu Pesto Zoodles

Preparation Time: 5 Minutes

Cooking Time: 12 Minutes

Servings: 4

Ingredients:

2 tbsp olive oil

1 medium white onion, chopped

1 garlic clove, minced

2 (14 oz) blocks firm tofu, soaked and cubed

1 medium red bell pepper, deseeded and sliced

6 medium zucchinis, spiralized

¼ cup basil pesto, olive oil-based

Salt and freshly ground black pepper to taste

½ cup shredded Gouda cheese

2/3 cup grated Parmesan cheese

Toasted pine nuts to garnish

Directions:

Over medium fire, heat olive oil in a medium pot and sauté onion and garlic until softened and fragrant, 3 minutes.

Add tofu and cook until golden on all sides. Pour in bell pepper and cook until softened, 4 minutes.

Mix in zucchinis, pesto, salt, and black pepper. Cook for 3 minutes or until zucchinis

soften slightly. Turn heat off and carefully mix in Gouda cheese to melt.

Dish into four plates, top with Parmesan cheese, pine nuts, and serve.

Nutrition:

Calories: 477 Cal Fat: 32 g

Carbs: 12.04 g Fiber: 6.6 g Protein: 20.42 g

36. Cheesy Mushroom Pie

Preparation Time: 10 Minutes

Cooking Time: 43 Minutes

Servings: 4

Ingredients:

For piecrust:

3 tbsp coconut flour

¼ cup almond flour + extra for dusting

½ tsp salt

¼ cup butter, cold and crumbled

3 tbsp swerve sugar

1 ½ tsp vanilla extract

4 whole eggs, cracked into a bowl

For filling:

2 tbsp butter

1 medium brown onion

2 garlic cloves, minced

1 green bell pepper, deseeded and diced

1 cup green beans, cut into 3 pieces each

2 cups mixed mushrooms, chopped

Salt and freshly ground black pepper to taste

¼ cup coconut cream

1/3 cup sour cream

½ cup unsweetened almond milk

2 eggs, lightly beaten

¼ tsp nutmeg powder

1 tbsp freshly chopped parsley

1 cup grated cheddar cheese

Directions:

For piecrust:

Preheat oven to 350oF and grease a pie pan with cooking spray. Set aside.

In a large bowl, combine coconut flour, almond flour, and salt.

Add butter and mix with an electric hand mixer until crumbly. Add swerve sugar, vanilla extract, and mix well. Pour in eggs one after another while mixing until formed into a ball.

Flatten dough on a chopping board, cover in plastic wrap, and refrigerate for 1 hour.

Lightly dust chopping board with almond flour, unwrap dough, and roll out into a large rectangle of ½-inch thickness. Fit dough in pie pan, and cover with parchment paper.

Pour in some baking beans and bake in oven until golden, 10 minutes. Remove after, pour out beans, remove parchment paper, and allow cooling.

For filling:

Meanwhile, melt butter in a skillet and sauté onion and garlic until softened and fragrant, 3 minutes. Add bell pepper, green beans, mushroom, salt and black pepper; cook for 5 minutes.

In a medium bowl, beat coconut cream, sour cream, almond milk, and eggs. Season with salt, black pepper, and nutmeg. Stir in parsley and cheddar cheese.

Spread mushroom mixture in baked crust and top with cheese filling.

Bake until golden on top and cheese melted, 20 to 25 minutes.

Remove; allow cooling for 10 minutes, slice, and serve.

Nutrition:

Calories: 527 Cal

Fat: 43.58 g

Carbs: 8.73 g

Fiber: 2.2 g

Protein: 21.3 g

37. Meatless Florentine Pizza

Preparation Time: 10 Minutes

Cooking Time: 25 Minutes

Servings: 2

Ingredients:

For pizza crust:

6 eggs

1 tsp Italian seasoning

1 cup shredded provolone cheese

For topping:

2/3 cup tomato sauce

2 cups baby spinach, wilted

½ cup grated mozzarella cheese

1 (7 oz) can sliced mushrooms, drained

4 eggs

Olive oil for drizzling

Directions:

For pizza crust:

Preheat oven to 400o F and line a pizza pan with parchment paper. Set aside.

Crack eggs into a medium bowl and whisk in Italian seasoning and provolone cheese.

Spread mixture on pizza pan and bake until golden, 10 minutes. Remove and allow cooling for 2 minutes.

For pizza:

Increase oven's temperature to 450o F.

Spread tomato sauce on crust, top with spinach, mozzarella cheese, and mushrooms. Bake for 8 minutes.

Crack eggs on top and continue baking until eggs set, 2 minutes.

Remove, slice, and serve.

Nutrition:

Calories: 646 Cal Fat: 39.19 g

Carbs: 8.42 g Fiber: 3.5 g Protein: 36.87 g

38. Margherita Pizza with Cauliflower Crust

Preparation Time: 8 Minutes

Cooking Time: 30 Minutes

Servings: 2

Ingredients:

For pizza crust:

2 cups cauliflower rice

4 eggs

¼ cup shredded Monterey Jack cheese

¼ cup shredded Parmesan cheese

½ tsp Italian seasoning

Salt and freshly ground black pepper to taste

For topping:

6 tbsp unsweetened tomato sauce

1 small red onion, thinly sliced

2 ½ oz cremini mushrooms, sliced

1 tsp dried oregano

½ cup cottage cheese

½ tbsp. olive oil

A handful fresh basil

Directions:

For pizza crust:

Preheat oven to 400o F and line a baking sheet with parchment paper.

Pour cauliflower into a safe microwave bowl, sprinkle with 1 tablespoon of water, cover with plastic wrap and microwave for 1 to 2 minutes or until softened. Remove and allow cooling.

Pour cauliflower into a cheesecloth and squeeze out as much liquid. Transfer to a mixing bowl.

Crack in eggs, add cheeses, Italian seasoning, salt, and black pepper. Mix until well-combined.

Spread mixture on baking sheet and bake in oven until golden, 15 minutes.

Remove from oven and allow cooling for 2 minutes.

For topping:

Spread tomato sauce on pizza crust, scatter onion and mushrooms on top, sprinkle with oregano, and add cottage cheese. Drizzle with olive oil and bake until golden, 15 minutes.

Remove, top with basil, slice and serve.

Nutrition:

Calories: 290 Cal Fat: 22.58 g

Carbs: 6.62 g Fiber: 5.8 g

Protein: 12.81 g

39. Almond Tofu Loaf

Preparation Time: 10 Minutes

Cooking Time: 1 Hour

Servings: 4

Ingredients:

3 tbsp olive oil + extra for brushing

4 garlic cloves, minced

2 white onions, finely chopped

1 lb. firm tofu, pressed and cubed

2 tbsp coconut aminos

¾ cup chopped almonds

Salt and freshly ground black pepper

1 tbsp dried mixed herbs

½ tsp erythritol

¼ cup golden flax seed meal

1 tbsp sesame seeds

1 cup chopped mixed bell peppers

½ cup tomato sauce

Directions:

Preheat oven to 350oF and lightly brush an 8 x 4-inch loaf pan with olive oil. Set aside.

In a medium bowl, combine olive oil, garlic, onion, tofu, coconut aminos, almonds, salt, black pepper, mixed herbs, erythritol, golden flax seed meal, sesame seeds, and bell peppers, and mix well.

Fit mixture in loaf pan, spread tomato sauce on top, and bake in oven for 45 minutes to 1 hour.

Remove pan and turn tofu loaf over onto a chopping board.

Slice and serve with garden green salad.

Nutrition:

Calories: 432 Cal

Fat: 31.38 g

Carbs: 8.74 g

Fiber: 6.2 g

Protein: 24.36 g

40. Kale and Mushroom Biryani

Preparation Time: 15 Minutes

Cooking Time: 46 Minutes

Servings: 4

Ingredients:

6 cups cauli rice

2 tbsp water

Salt and freshly ground black pepper

3 tbsp ghee

3 medium white onions, chopped

1 tsp ginger puree

1 tbsp turmeric powder + more for dusting

2 cups chopped tomatoes

1 red chili, finely chopped

1 tbsp tomato puree

1 cup sliced cremini mushrooms

1 cup diced paneer cheese

1 cup kale, chopped

1/3 cup water

1 cup plain yogurt

¼ cup chopped cilantro

Olive oil for drizzling

Directions:

Preheat oven to 400o F.

Pour cauliflower rice into a safe microwave bowl, drizzle with water, cover with plastic wrap, and microwave for 1 minute or until softened. Remove and season with salt and black pepper. Set aside.

Melt ghee in a casserole pan and sauté onion, ginger, and turmeric powder. Cook until fragrant, 5 minutes.

Add tomatoes, red chili, and tomato puree; cook until tomatoes soften, 5 minutes.

Stir in mushrooms, paneer cheese, kale, and water; season with salt and black pepper and simmer until mushrooms soften, 10 minutes. Turn heat off and stir in yogurt.

Spoon half of stew into a bowl and set aside. Sprinkle half of cilantro on remaining stew in casserole pan, top with half of cauli rice, and dust with turmeric. Repeat layering a second time with remaining ingredients.

Drizzle with olive oil and bake until golden and crisp on top, 25 minutes.

Remove; allow cooling, and serve with coconut chutney.

Nutrition:

Calories: 346 Cal Fat: 21.48 g

Carbs: 8.63 g Fiber: 6.6 g

Protein: 16.01 g

41. Mushroom Pizza Bowls with Avocado & Cilantro

Preparation Time: 15 Minutes

Cooking Time: 17 Minutes

Servings: 4

Ingredients: 1 ½ cups broccoli rice

2 tbsp water

Olive oil for brushing

2 cups unsweetened pizza sauce

1 cup grated Gruyere cheese

1 cup grated mozzarella cheese

2 large tomatoes, chopped

½ cup sliced cremini mushrooms

1 small red onion, chopped

1 tsp dried basil

Salt and freshly ground black pepper to taste

1 avocado, halved, pitted, and chopped

¼ cup chopped parsley

Directions:

Preheat oven to 400o F.

Pour broccoli rice into a safe microwave bowl, drizzle with water, and steam in microwave for 1 to 2 minutes. Remove, fluff with a fork, and set aside.

Lightly brush the inner parts of four medium ramekins with olive oil and spread in half of pizza sauce. Top with half of broccoli rice and half of cheeses.

In a bowl, combine tomatoes, mushrooms, onion, basil, salt, and black pepper. Spoon half of mixture into ramekins and top with half of cheeses. Repeat layering a second time making sure to finish off with cheeses.

Bake until cheese melts and golden on top, 15 minutes.

Remove ramekins and top with avocados and parsley.

Allow cooling for 3 minutes and serve.

Nutrition:

Calories: 378 Cal Fat: 22.54 g

Carbs: 12.27 g Fiber: 8.9 g Protein: 20.68 g

42. Pistachios and Cheese Stuffed Zucchinis

Preparation Time: 15 Minutes

Cooking Time: 17 Minutes

Servings: 4

Ingredients: 1 cup rice broccoli

¼ cup vegetable broth

4 medium zucchinis, halved

2 tbsp olive oil + more for drizzling

1 ¼ cup diced tomatoes

1 medium red onion, chopped

¼ cup pine nuts ¼ cup chopped pistachios

4 tbsp chopped parsley

1 tbsp smoked paprika

1 tbsp balsamic vinegar

Salt and freshly ground black pepper to taste

1 cup grated Parmesan cheese

Directions:

Preheat oven to 350oF.

Pour broccoli rice and vegetable broth in a medium pot and cook over medium heat until softened, 2 minutes. Turn heat off, fluff broccoli rice, and allow cooling.

Scoop flesh out of zucchini halves, chop pulp and set aside. Brush zucchini boats with some olive oil. Set aside.

In a medium bowl, combine broccoli rice, tomatoes, red onion, pine nuts, pistachios, parsley, paprika, balsamic vinegar, zucchini pulp, salt, and black pepper.

Spoon mixture into zucchini boats, drizzle with more olive oil, and cover top with Parmesan cheese.

Place filled zucchinis on a baking sheet and bake until cheese melts and is golden, 15 minutes.

Remove, allow cooling, and serve.

Nutrition: Calories: 330 CalFat: 28.12 g

Carbs: 10.62 g Fiber: 5.4 g Protein: 12.3 g

43. Soy Chorizo-Asparagus Bowl

Preparation Time: 15 Minutes

Cooking Time: 15 Minutes

Servings: 4

Ingredients:

1 lb. soy chorizo, cubed

1 lb. asparagus, trimmed and halved

1 cup green beans, trimmed

1 cup chopped mixed bell peppers

2 red onions, cut into wedges

1 head medium broccoli, cut into florets

2 rosemary sprigs

Salt and freshly ground black pepper to taste

4 tbsp olive oil

1 tbsp maple (sugar-free) syrup

1 lemon, juiced

Directions:

Preheat oven to 400o F.

On a baking tray, spread soy chorizo, asparagus, green beans, bell peppers, onions, broccoli, and rosemary. Season with salt, black pepper, and drizzle with olive oil and maple syrup. Rub spices into vegetables.

Bake until vegetables soften and light brown around the edges, 15 minutes.

Dish vegetables into serving bowls, drizzle with lemon juice, and serve warm.

Nutrition:

Calories: 300 Cal Fat: 18.55 g Carbs: 12.5 g

Fiber: 9.2 g Protein: 14.87 g

44. Creamy Brussels Sprouts Bowls

Preparation Time: 10 Minutes

Cooking Time: 30 Minutes

Servings: 4

Ingredients: 1 tablespoon olive oil

1-pound Brussels sprouts, trimmed and halved

1 cup coconut cream

½ teaspoon chili powder

½ teaspoon garam masala

½ teaspoon garlic powder

A pinch of salt and black pepper

1 tablespoon lime juice

Directions: 2In a roasting pan, combine the sprouts with the cream, chili powder and the other ingredients, toss, introduce in the oven at 380 degrees F and bake for 30 minutes. Divide into bowls and serve for lunch.

Nutrition: Calories: 219 Cal Fat: 18.3 g

Fiber: 5.7 g Carbs: 14.1 Protein: 5.4 g

45. Green Beans and Radishes Bake

Preparation Time: 10 Minutes

Cooking Time: 25 Minutes

Servings: 4

Ingredients:

2 tablespoons olive oil

1-pound green beans, trimmed and halved

2 cups radishes, sliced

1 cup coconut cream

1 teaspoon sweet paprika

1 cup cashew cheese, shredded

Salt and black pepper to the taste

1 tablespoon chives, chopped

Directions:

In a roasting pan, combine the green beans with the radishes and the other ingredients except the cheese and toss.

Sprinkle the cheese on top, introduce in the oven at 375 degrees F and bake for 25 minutes.

Divide the mix between plates and serve.

Nutrition: Calories: 130 Cal

Fat: 1 g Fiber: 0.4 g

Carbs: 1 g Protein: 0.1 g

46. Avocado and Radish Bowls

Preparation Time: 10 Minutes

Cooking Time: 0

Servings: 4

Ingredients:

2 cups radishes, halved

2 avocados, peeled, pitted and roughly cubed

2 tablespoons coconut cream

2 tablespoons balsamic vinegar

1 tablespoon green onion, chopped

1 teaspoon chili powder

1 cup baby spinach

Salt and black pepper to the taste

Directions:

In a bowl, combine the radishes with the avocados and the other ingredients, toss, divide into smaller bowls and serve for lunch.

Nutrition:

Calories: 340 Cal

Fat: 23

Fiber: 3 g

Carbs: 6 g

Protein: 5 g

47. Celery and Radish Soup

Preparation Time: 10 Minutes

Cooking Time: 20 Minutes

Servings: 4

Ingredients:

½ pound radishes, cut into quarters

2 celery stalks, chopped

2 tablespoons olive oil

4 scallions, chopped

1 teaspoon fennel seeds, crushed

1 teaspoon coriander, dried

6 cups vegetable stock

Salt and black pepper to the taste

6 garlic cloves, minced

1 tablespoon chives, chopped

Directions:

Heat up a pot with the oil over medium heat, add the celery, scallions and the garlic and sauté for 5 minutes.

Add the radishes and the other ingredients, bring to a boil, cover and simmer for 15 minutes.

Divide into soup bowls and serve.

Nutrition:

Calories: 120 Cal Fat: 2 g

Fiber: 1 g Carbs: 3 g Protein: 10 g

48. Lime Avocado and Cucumber Soup

Preparation Time: 5 Minutes

Cooking Time: 0 Minutes

Servings: 4

Ingredients: 1 tablespoon olive oil

2 avocados, pitted, peeled and roughly cubed

2 cucumbers, sliced   4 cups vegetable stock

Salt and black pepper to the taste

¼ teaspoon lemon zest, grated

1 tablespoon white vinegar

1 cup scallions, chopped

¼ cup cilantro, chopped

Directions: In a blender, combine the avocados with the cucumbers and the other ingredients, pulse well, divide into bowls and serve for lunch.

Nutrition: Calories: 100 Cal

Fat: 10 g Fiber: 2 g Carbs: 5 g Protein: 8 g

49. Avocado and Kale Soup

Preparation Time: 5 Minutes

Cooking Time: 7 Minutes

Servings: 4

Ingredients:

4 cups kale, torn

1 teaspoon turmeric powder

1 avocado, pitted, peeled and sliced

4 cups vegetable stock

Juice of 1 lime

2 garlic cloves, minced

1 tablespoon chives, chopped

Salt and black pepper to the taste

Directions:

In a pot, combine the kale with the avocado and the other ingredients, bring to a simmer, cook over medium heat for 7 minutes, blend using an immersion blender, divide into bowls and serve.

Nutrition:

Calories: 234 Cal

Fat: 4 g

Carbs: 7 g

Protein :12

50. Spinach and Cucumber Salad

Preparation Time: 5 Minutes

Cooking Time: 0

Servings: 4

Ingredients:

1-pound cucumber, sliced

2 cups baby spinach

1 tablespoon chili powder

2 tablespoons olive oil

¼ cup cilantro, chopped

2 tablespoons lemon juice

Salt and black pepper to the taste

Directions:

In a large salad bowl, combine the cucumber with the spinach and the other ingredients, toss and serve for lunch.

Nutrition:

Calories: 140 Cal

Fat: 4 g

Fiber: 2 g

Carbs: 4 g

Protein: 5 g

Snack Recipes

51. Nori Snack Rolls

Preparation Time: 5 Minutes

Cooking Time: 10 Minutes

Servings: 4

Ingredients

2 tablespoons almond, cashew, peanut, or other nut butter

2 tablespoons tamari, or soy sauce

4 standard nori sheets

1 mushroom, sliced

1 tablespoon pickled ginger

½ cup grated carrots

Directions

Preheat the oven to 350°F.

Mix together the nut butter and tamari until smooth and very thick. Lay out a nori sheet, rough side up, the long way.

Spread a thin line of the tamari mixture on the far end of the nori sheet, from side to side. Lay the mushroom slices, ginger, and carrots in a line at the other end (the end closest to you).

Fold the vegetables inside the nori, rolling toward the tahini mixture, which will seal the roll. Repeat to make 4 rolls.

Put on a baking sheet and bake for 8 to 10 minutes, or until the rolls are slightly browned and crispy at the ends. Let the rolls cool for a few minutes, then slice each roll into 3 smaller pieces.

Nutrition

Calories: 79 Cal Fat: 5 g

Carbs: 6 gFiber: 2 g Protein: 4 g

52. Risotto Bites

Preparation Time: 15 Minutes

Cooking Time: 20 Minutes

Servings: 12

Ingredients

½ cup panko bread crumbs

1 teaspoon paprika

1 teaspoon chipotle powder or ground cayenne pepper

1½ cups cold Green Pea Risotto

Nonstick cooking spray

Directions

Preheat the oven to 425°F.

Line a baking sheet with parchment paper.

On a large plate, combine the panko, paprika, and chipotle powder. Set aside.

Roll 2 tablespoons of the risotto into a ball.

Gently roll in the bread crumbs, and place on the prepared baking sheet. Repeat to make a total of 12 balls.

Spritz the tops of the risotto bites with nonstick cooking spray and bake for 15 to 20 minutes, until they begin to brown. Cool completely before storing in a large airtight container in a single layer (add a piece of parchment paper for a second layeror in a plastic freezer bag.

Nutrition:

Calories: 100 Cal

Fat: 2 g

Protein: 6 g

Carbs: 17 g

Fiber: 5 g

53. Jicama and Guacamole

Preparation Time: 15 Minutes

Cooking Time: 0

Servings: 4

Ingredients

juice of 1 lime, or 1 tablespoon prepared lime juice

2 hass avocados, peeled, pits removed, and cut into cubes

½ teaspoon sea salt

½ red onion, minced

1 garlic clove, minced

¼ cup chopped cilantro (optional

1 jicama bulb, peeled and cut into matchsticks

Directions

In a medium bowl, squeeze the lime juice over the top of the avocado and sprinkle with salt.

Lightly mash the avocado with a fork. Stir in the onion, garlic, and cilantro, if using.

Serve with slices of jicama to dip in guacamole.

To store, place plastic wrap over the bowl of guacamole and refrigerate. The guacamole will keep for about 2 days.

Nutrition:

Calories: 130 Cal Fat: 2 g Protein: 5 g

Carbs: 13 g Fiber: 5 g

54. Curried Tofu "Egg Salad" Pitas

Preparation Time: 15 Minutes

Cooking Time: 0 Minutes

Servings: 4 Sandwiches

Ingredients

1-pound extra-firm tofu, drained and patted dry

1/2 cup vegan mayonnaise, homemade or store-bought

1/4 cup chopped mango chutney, homemade or store-bought

2 teaspoons Dijon mustard

1 tablespoon hot or mild curry powder

1 teaspoon salt

1/8 teaspoon ground cayenne

¾ cup shredded carrots

2 celery ribs, minced

1/4 cup minced red onion

8 small Boston or other soft lettuce leaves

4 (7-inchwhole wheat pita breads, halved

Directions

Crumble the tofu and place it in a large bowl. Add the mayonnaise, chutney, mustard, curry powder, salt, and cayenne, and stir well until thoroughly mixed.

Add the carrots, celery, and onion and stir to combine. Refrigerate for 30 minutes to allow the flavors to blend.

Tuck a lettuce leaf inside each pita pocket, spoon some tofu mixture on top of the lettuce, and serve.

Nutrition:

Calories: 200 CalFat: 3 g Protein: 9 g

Carbs: 11 g Fiber: 8 g

55. Garden Patch Sandwiches on Multigrain Bread

Preparation Time: 15 Minutes

Cooking Time: 0 Minutes

Servings: 4 Sandwiches

Ingredients

1pound extra-firm tofu, drained and patted dry

1 medium red bell pepper, finely chopped

1 celery rib, finely chopped

3 green onions, minced

1/4 cup shelled sunflower seeds

1/2 cup vegan mayonnaise, homemade or store-bought

1/2 teaspoon salt

1/2 teaspoon celery salt

1/4 teaspoon freshly ground black pepper

8 slices whole grain bread

4 (1/4-inchslices ripe tomato

4 lettuce leaves

Directions

Crumble the tofu and place it in a large bowl. Add the bell pepper, celery, green onions, and sunflower seeds. Stir in the mayonnaise, salt, celery salt, and pepper and mix until well combined.

Toast the bread, if desired. Spread the mixture evenly onto 4 slices of the bread. Top each with a tomato slice, lettuce leaf, and the remaining bread. Cut the sandwiches diagonally in half and serve.

Nutrition:

Calories: 234 Cal Fat: 6 g

Protein: 3 g Carbs: 12 g Fiber: 9 g

56. Garden Salad Wraps

Preparation Time: 15 Minutes

Cooking Time: 10 Minutes

Servings: 4 Wraps

Ingredients 6 tablespoons olive oil

1-pound extra-firm tofu, drained, patted dry, and cut into 1/2-inch strips

1 tablespoon soy sauce

1/4 cup apple cider vinegar

1 teaspoon yellow or spicy brown mustard

1/2 teaspoon salt

1/4 teaspoon freshly ground black pepper

3 cups shredded romaine lettuce

3 ripe Roma tomatoes, finely chopped

1 large carrot, shredded

1 medium English cucumber, peeled and chopped

1/3 cup minced red onion

1/4 cup sliced pitted green olives

4 (10-inchwhole-grain flour tortillas or lavash flatbread

Directions

In a large skillet, heat 2 tablespoons of the oil over medium heat. Add the tofu and cook until golden brown, about 10 minutes. Sprinkle with soy sauce and set aside to cool. In a small bowl, combine the vinegar, mustard, salt, and pepper with the remaining 4 tablespoons oil, stirring to blend well. Set aside. In a large bowl, combine the lettuce, tomatoes, carrot, cucumber, onion, and olives. Pour on the dressing and toss to coat. To assemble wraps, place 1 tortilla on a work surface and spread with about one-quarter of the salad. Place a few strips of tofu on the tortilla and roll up tightly. Slice in half

Nutrition: Calories: 200 Cal Fat: 5 g

Protein: 6 g Carbs: 7 g Fiber: 7 g

57. Black Sesame Wonton Chips

Preparation Time: 5 Minutes

Cooking Time: 5 Minutes

Servings: 6

Ingredients

12 Vegan Wonton Wrappers

Toasted sesame oil

1/3 cup black sesame seeds

Salt

Directions

Preheat the oven to 450°F. Lightly oil a baking sheet and set aside. Cut the wonton wrappers in half crosswise, brush them with sesame oil, and arrange them in a single layer on the prepared baking sheet.

Sprinkle wonton wrappers with the sesame seeds and salt to taste, and bake until crisp and golden brown, 5 to 7 minutes. Cool completely before serving. These are best eaten on the day they are made but, once cooled, they can be covered and stored at room temperature for 1 to 2 days.

Nutrition:

Calories: 150 Cal

Fat: 2 g

Protein : 8 g

Carbs: 11 g

Fiber: 9 g

58. Marinated Mushroom Wraps

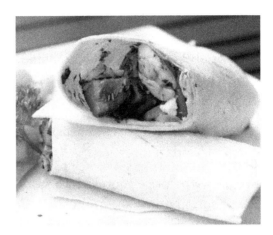

Preparation time: 15 minutes

cooking time: 0 minutes

servings: 2

Ingredients

3 tablespoons soy sauce

3 tablespoons fresh lemon juice

11/2 tablespoons toasted sesame oil

2 portobello mushroom caps, cut into 1/4-inch strips

1 ripe Hass avocado, pitted and peeled

2 (10-inchwhole-grain flour tortillas

2 cups fresh baby spinach leaves

1 medium red bell pepper, cut into 1/4-inch strips

1 ripe tomato, chopped

Salt and freshly ground black pepper

Directions

In a medium bowl, combine the soy sauce, 2 tablespoons of the lemon juice, and the oil. Add the portobello strips, toss to combine, and marinate for 1 hour or overnight. Drain the mushrooms and set aside.

Mash the avocado with the remaining 1 tablespoon of lemon juice.

To assemble wraps, place 1 tortilla on a work surface and spread with some of the mashed avocado. Top with a layer of baby spinach leaves. In the lower third of each tortilla, arrange strips of the soaked mushrooms and some of the bell pepper strips. Sprinkle with the tomato and salt and black pepper to taste. Roll up tightly and cut in half diagonally. Repeat with the remaining Ingredients and serve.

Nutrition:

Calories: 143 Cal

Fat: 3g

Protein: 16 g

Carbs: 7 g

Fiber: 3 g

59. Tamari Toasted Almonds

Preparation Time: 2 Minutes

Cooking Time: 8 Minutes

Servings: 1

Ingredients

½ cup raw almonds, or sunflower seeds

2 tablespoons tamari, or soy sauce

1 teaspoon toasted sesame oil

Directions

Heat a dry skillet to medium-high heat, then add the almonds, stirring very frequently to keep them from burning. Once the almonds are toasted, 7 to 8 minutes for almonds, or 3 to 4 minutes for sunflower seeds, pour the tamari and sesame oil into the hot skillet and stir to coat.

You can turn off the heat, and as the almonds cool the tamari mixture will stick to and dry on the nuts.

Nutrition:

Calories: 89 Cal

fat: 8 g

Carbs: 3 g

Fiber: 2 g

Protein: 4 g

60. Avocado and Tempeh Bacon Wraps

Preparation Time: 10 Minutes

Cooking Time: 8 Minutes

Servings: 4

Ingredients 2 tablespoons olive oil

8 ounces tempeh bacon, homemade or store-bought

4 (10-inchsoft flour tortillas or lavash flat bread

1/4 cup vegan mayonnaise, homemade or store-bought - 4 large lettuce leaves

2 ripe Hass avocados, pitted, peeled, and cut into 1/4-inch slices

1 large ripe tomato, cut into 1/4-inch slices

Directions

In a large skillet, heat the oil over medium heat. Add the tempeh bacon and cook until browned on both sides, about 8 minutes. Remove from the heat and set aside.

Place 1 tortilla on a work surface. Spread with some of t he mayonnaise and one-fourth of the lettuce and tomatoes.

Pit, peel, and thinly slice the avocado and place the slices on top of the tomato. Add the reserved tempeh bacon and roll up tightly. Repeat with remaining Ingredients and serve.

Nutrition: Calories: 132 Cal Fat: 1 g

Protein: 8 g Carbs: 12 g Fiber: 2 g

61. Kale Chips

Preparation Time: 5 Minutes

Cooking Time: 25 Minutes

Servings: 2

Ingredients

1 large bunch kale

1 tablespoon extra-virgin olive oil

½ teaspoon chipotle powder

½ teaspoon smoked paprika

¼ teaspoon salt

Directions

Preheat the oven to 275°F.

Line a large baking sheet with parchment paper. In a large bowl, stem the kale and tear it into bite-size pieces. Add the olive oil, chipotle powder, smoked paprika, and salt.

Toss the kale with tongs or your hands, coating each piece well.

Spread the kale over the parchment paper in a single layer.

Bake for 25 minutes, turning halfway through, until crisp.

Cool for 10 to 15 minutes before dividing and storing in 2 airtight containers.

Nutrition:

Calories: 144 Cal Fat: 7 g Protein: 5 g

Carbs: 18 g Fiber: 3 g

62. Tempeh-Pimiento Cheese Ball

Preparation Time: 5 Minutes

Cooking Time: 30 Minutes

Servings: 8

Ingredients ¾ cup chopped pecans

8 ounces tempeh, cut into 1/2-inch pieces

1 (2-ouncejar chopped pimientos, drained

1/4 cup nutritional yeast

1/4 cup vegan mayonnaise, homemade or store-bought

2 tablespoons soy sauce

Directions

In a medium saucepan of simmering water, cook the tempeh for 30 minutes. Set aside to cool. In a food processor, combine the cooled tempeh, pimientos, nutritional yeast, mayo, and soy sauce. Process until smooth. Transfer the tempeh mixture to a bowl and refrigerate until firm and chilled, at least 2 hours or overnight. In a dry skillet, toast the pecans over medium heat until lightly toasted, about 5 minutes. Set aside to cool. Shape the temp eh mixture into a ball, and roll it in the pecans, pressin g the nuts slightly into the tempeh mixture so they stick. Refrigerate for at least 1 hour before serving. If not using right away, cover and keep refrigerated until needed. Properly stored, it will keep for 2 to 3 days.

Nutrition: Calories: 188 Cal Fat: 3 g

Protein: 4 g Carbs: 19 g Fiber: 8 g

63. Seaweed Crackers

Preparation Time: 10 Minutes

Cooking Time: 24 Hours

Servings: 4

Ingredients:

1/2 cup flax seeds

1/2 cup golden flax seeds

1 1/2 cups water

2 tablespoon gluten-free tamari

2 nori sheets, broken up

Directions:

Soak tamari and flaxseeds in water in a bowl for 1 hour.

Add nori to this water and mix well.

Add 1 tablespoon of this mixture per cracker over Teflon sheet.

Place this sheet in the dehydrator and cook for 24 hours at 110 degrees F.

Flip the crackers after 12 hours.

Serve fresh.

Nutrition:

Calories: 221 Cal

Fat: 7.3 g Carbs: 3 g

Protein: 14.2 g

64. Sesame Tamari Almonds

Preparation Time: 10 Minutes

Cooking Time: 5 Minutes

Servings: 4

Ingredients:

4 teaspoons toasted sesame oil

3 tablespoons low sodium gluten-free tamari

2 pinches of salt

1/4 teaspoon swerve

2 cups of raw almonds

2 tablespoons sesame seeds

Directions:

Mix tamari, salt, sesame oil and stevia in a small bowl.

Toast almonds in a nonstick skillet then add sesame tamari mixture.

Stir cook for 5 minutes.

Drizzle sesame seeds over them.

Enjoy fresh.

Nutrition:

Calories: 152 Cal

Fat: 31.3 g

Carbs: 2.7 g

Protein: 3.7 g

65. Edamame Avocado Hummus

Preparation Time: 10 Minutes

Cooking Time: 0

Servings: 6

Ingredients:

1 clove garlic minced

12 oz. bag shelled edamame soybeans

1/4 cup tahini

1/4 cup lemon juice

1/2 cup avocado

1/4 cup water or more if desired

2 tablespoons olive oil

salt and pepper

Directions:

Add everything to a blender jug.

Pulse well until smooth.

Serve the hummus with low car crackers.

Nutrition:

Calories: 166 Cal

Fat: 11.4 g

Carbohydrates: 6.6 g

Protein: 2.4 g

66. Pizza Cheese Ball

Preparation Time: 10 Minutes

Cooking Time: 0

Servings: 4

Ingredients: 1 (8 ounces) cream cheese

1 (10 ounces) vegetarian mozzarella

1/4 cup sun-dried tomatoes

1/4 cup green olives

1 teaspoon basil 1 teaspoon oregano

1/2 teaspoon garlic powder

1/2 teaspoon onion powder

1 teaspoon red pepper flakes

Salt and pepper 1/4 cup walnuts chopped

Directions:

Slice the mozzarella block into thin strips. Grind walnuts in a food processor and spread them in a plate.

Blend all the remaining ingredients for the ball in the blender.

Make small balls out of this mixture then roll them in walnuts.

Wrap the cheese strips over the cheese balls.

Enjoy fresh.

Nutrition:

Calories: 94 Cal Fat: 7 g

Carbs: 5 g Protein: 1 g

67. Tahini Keto Bagels

Preparation Time: 10 minutes

Cooking Time: 40 minutes

Servings: 4

Ingredients: 1/2 cup ground flax seed

1/2 cup tahini 1/4 cup psyllium husks

1 cup of water 1 teaspoon baking powder

pinch of salt

sesame seeds for garnish

Directions:

Let your oven preheat at 375 degrees F.

Whisk psyllium husk with baking powder, flaxseeds, and salt in a mixing bowl.

Mix tahini with water in a separate bowl until well combined.

Add the husk mixture to make a dough. Knead well over the working surface.

Make 4 inches in diameter patties with ¼ inch thickness.

Place the prepared patties on the baking tray and drizzle sesame seeds over them.

Bake the patties for 40 minutes in the set oven until golden brown.

Enjoy fresh.

Nutrition: Calories: 79 Cal Fat: 4.3 g

Carbs: 7.1 g Protein: 2.6 g

68. Zucchini Nests

Preparation Time: 10 Minutes

Cooking Time: 10 Minutes

Servings: 4

Ingredients:

3 large zucchinis, spiralized

1 teaspoon of sea salt

1/4 teaspoon garlic powder

1/4 teaspoon onion powder

1/8 teaspoon ground black pepper

4 large eggs

Coconut oil, for greasing

Directions:

Pass the zucchini through the spiralizer cutter to make its thin noodles.

Place the noodles in a colander and sprinkle salt over th em then leave them for 20 minutes.

Let your oven preheat at 400 degrees and grease a muffin tin with coconut oil.

Squeeze all the water out the noodles by pressing them firmly.

Mix black pepper, onion powder and garlic powder in a large bowl.

Toss in zucchini noodles and mix well to coat.

Divide the noodles into the muffin cups and make a nest at the center of each muffin cup.

Crack one egg at the center of each nest.

Drizzle salt and pepper on top.

Bake for 10 minutes until it's done.

Serve fresh.

Nutrition: Calories: 155 Cal

Fat: 2.1 g Carbs: 5.9 g Protein: 12.6 g

69. Low Carb Bibimbap

Preparation Time: 10 Minutes

Cooking Time: 10 Minutes

Servings: 4

Ingredients: 1 tablespoon soy sauce

2 tablespoons rice vinegar

7 oz tempeh, sliced into squares

1 small red bell pepper, in strips

4-6 broccoli florets, in thin spears

1 carrot, grated 1/2 cucumber, in strips

10 oz raw cauliflower, riced

2 tablespoons chili paste

2 tablespoons rice vinegar

1 tablespoon soy sauce

1 teaspoon sesame oil

concentrated liquid sweetener to taste

2 tablespoons sesame seeds

Directions:

Whisk soy sauce with vinegar in a bowl then toss in tempeh squares.

Let them sit for 1 minute and meanwhile dice the vegetables. Warm oil in a skillet and sauté tempeh in it for 4 minutes on medium heat.

Transfer the tempeh to a plate then add broccoli, carrots, and peppers. Cover the skillet and cook for 2 minutes. Sauté caulifl ower rice in a separate pan until soft.

Mix soy sauce with chili paste, oil, and sweetener in a small bowl.

Toss cauliflower rice with tempeh, peppers, broccoli, carrot, and cucumber in a salad bowl.

Stir in chili paste mixture and mix well to coat. Garnish with sesame seeds.

Enjoy fresh.

Nutrition: Calories: 164 Cal

Fat: 10.3 g Carbohydrates: 4 g Protein: 1.4 g

70. Walnut Carrot Bombs

Preparation Time: 10 Minutes

Cooking Time: 45 Minutes

Servings: 6

Ingredients: 1/2 cup raw walnut

3 medium carrots, peeled and grated

2 cloves garlic, minced

Salt and pepper, to taste

1 tablespoon cream cheese

1 tablespoon heavy cream

1/2 cup shredded Parmesan cheese

Directions:

Let your oven preheat at 350 degrees F and layer a muffin tin with cooking oil. Grate carrots by grinding them in a food processor on high speed. Add walnuts and grind again to make a crumbly mixture.

Stir in cheese, cream cheese, cream, salt, garlic, and black pepper. Blend again until evenly mixed. Make small golf ball sized balls out of this mixture.

Place each ball in the muffin cups and bake them for 45 minutes until golden brown.

Allow it to cool for 5 minutes approximately then serve fresh.

Nutrition: Calories: 118 Cal

Fat: 18.3 g Carbs: 9 g Protein: 5.1 g

71. Nutty Zucchini Salad

Preparation Time: 10 Minutes

Cooking Time: 3 Minutes

Servings: 2

Ingredients:

1/4 cup pine nuts

2 tablespoons butter

1 large zucchini, julienned

Salt to taste

2 tablespoons Parmesan cheese, grated

Directions:

Add and melt butter in a large skillet over medium heat then toss in pine nuts.

Stir cook for 3 minutes until golden brown.

Add zucchini and sauté for few seconds then add salt to adjust seasoning.

Garnish with parmesan then serve fresh.

Nutrition:

Calories: 102 Cal

Fat: 17.3 g

Carbs: 6.1 g

Protein: 1.2 g

72. Kale Pate Spread

Preparation Time: 10 Minutes

Cooking Time: 7 Minutes

Servings: 6

Ingredients:

6 cups green kale, chopped

1 tablespoon olive oil

½ cup raw organic sesame seeds

½ cup extra-virgin olive oil

8 green onions, green parts only

3 tablespoon apple cider vinegar

1 ¼ teaspoon grey sea salt

Directions:

Mix kale with a tablespoon of olive oil and cook it under the lid for 7 minutes in a skillet on low heat.

Transfer the kale to a food processor along with all the remaining ingredients.

Pulse to make a smooth mixture then transfer it to a mason jar.

Refrigerate and store for 4 days.

Serve it with low carb crackers.

Nutrition:

Calories: 61 Cal Fat: 21.2 g

Carbs: 6 g Protein: 4.1 g

73. Smoked Almonds

Preparation Time: 5 Minutes

Cooking Time: 45 Minutes

Servings: 10

Ingredients: 1-pound raw almonds

2 tablespoons grass-fed butter, melted

2 tablespoons liquid smoke

2 tablespoons Worcestershire sauce

1 tablespoon salt

Directions:

Preheat the oven to 200°F. Line a baking dish with aluminum foil.

Put the almonds in a large mixing bowl and set aside.

In a sm all bowl, mix together the butter, liquid smoke, and Worcestershire sauce.

Pour the mixture over the almonds and stir. Sprinkle in the salt and mix again.

Spread the almonds evenly on the prepared baking dish and place in the oven.

Coo k for 45 minutes, stirring well every 10 minutes. Once cooked, transfer the nuts to paper towels to drain. When cool, store in an airtight container until ready to serve.

Nutrition:

Calories: 305 Cal Fat: 25 g

Protein: 10 g Carbs: 10 g Fiber: 6 g

74. Roasted Garlic Mushrooms

Preparation Time: 5 Minutes

Cooking Time: 25 Minutes

Servings: 4

Ingredients: ½ teaspoon salt

Nonstick cooking spray

1⅓ pounds cremini mushrooms

6 garlic cloves, minced

3 tablespoons avocado oil

3 tablespoons Parmesan cheese

¼ teaspoon freshly ground black pepper

3 tablespoons dried parsley

Directions:

Preheat the oven to 400°F. Line a baking sheet with aluminum foil and spray with nonstick cooking spray.

In a mixing bowl, combine the mushrooms, garlic, avocado oil, Parmesan cheese, salt, and pepper. Mix well.

Spread the mushroom mixture on the prepared baking sheet and sprinkle with the parsley.

Bake for 12 minutes and stir. Return to the oven and bake for an additional 12 minutes.

Transfer the mushrooms to a serving dish.

Nutrition: Calories: 180 Cal Fat: 13 g

Protein: 8 g Carbs: 8 g Fiber: 1 g

75. Mediterranean Cucumber Bites

Preparation Time: 10 Minutes

Cooking Time: 0

Servings: 4

Ingredients:

8 ounces cream cheese, at room temperature

2 tablespoons chopped flat-leaf parsley

⅓ cup diced black olives

1 bell pepper, diced

2 cucumbers, halved lengthwise and seeded

2 tablespoons sliced scallions

Directions:

In a small bowl, mix together the cream cheese, parsley, olives, and bell pepper.

Fill each cucumber cavity with the cream cheese mixture. Sprinkle with the scallions, slice into 1-inch pieces, and serve.

Nutrition:

Calories: 253 Cal

Fat: 21 g

Protein: 6 g

Carbs: 10 g

Fiber: 2 g

Dinner Recipes

76. Seitan Tex-Mex Casserole

Preparation Time: 5 Minutes

Cooking Time: 35 Minutes

Servings: 4

Ingredients:

2 tbsp vegan butter

1 ½ lb seitan

3 tbsp Tex-Mex seasoning

2 tbsp chopped jalapeño peppers

½ cup crushed tomatoes

Salt and black pepper to taste

½ cup shredded vegan cheese

1 tbsp chopped fresh green onion to garnish

1 cup sour cream for serving

Directions:

Preheat the oven and grease a baking dish with cooking spray. Set aside.

Melt the vegan butter in a medium skillet over medium heat and cook the seitan until brown, 10 minutes.

Stir in the Tex-Mex seasoning, jalapeño peppers, and tomatoes; simmer for 5 minutes and adjust the taste with salt and black pepper.

Transfer and level the mixture in the baking dish. Top with the vegan cheese and bake in the upper rack of the oven for 15 to 20 minutes or until the cheese melts and is golden brown.

Remove the dish and garnish with the green onion.

Serve the casserole with sour cream.

Nutrition:

Calories: 464 Cal

Fat:37.8 g

Carbs: 12 g

Fiber: 2 g

Protein: 24 g

77. Avocado Coconut Pie

Preparation Time: 30 Minutes

Cooking Time: 50 Minutes

Servings: 4

Ingredients:

For the piecrust:

1 tbsp flax seed powder + 3 tbsp water

4 tbsp coconut flour

4 tbsp chia seeds

¾ cup almond flour

1 tbsp psyllium husk powder

1 tsp baking powder

1 pinch salt

3 tbsp coconut oil

4 tbsp water

For the filling:

2 ripe avocados

1 cup vegan mayonnaise

3 tbsp flax seed powder + 9 tbsp water

2 tbsp fresh parsley, finely chopped

1 jalapeno, finely chopped

½ tsp onion powder

¼ tsp salt

½ cup cashew cream

1¼ cups shredded tofu cheese

Directions:

In 2 separate bowls, mix the different portions of flax seed powder with the respective quantity of water. Allow absorbing for 5 minutes.

Preheat the oven to 350 F.

In a food processor, add the coconut flour, chia seeds, almond flour, psyllium husk powder, baking powder, salt, coconut oil, water, and the smaller portion of the flax egg. Blend the ingredients until the resulting dough forms into a ball.

Line a spring form pan with about 12-inch diameter of parchment paper and spread the dough in the pan. Bake for 10 to 15 minutes or until a light golden brown color is achieved.

Meanwhile, cut the avocado into halves lengthwise, remove the pit, and chop the pulp. Put in a bowl and add the mayonnaise, remaining flax egg, parsley, jalapeno, onion powder, salt, cashew cream, and tofu cheese. Combine well.

Remove the piecrust when ready and fill with the creamy mixture. Level the filling with a spatula and continue baking for 35 minutes or until lightly golden brown.

When ready, take out. Cool before slicing and serving with a baby spinach salad.

Nutrition:

Calories:680 Cal

Fat:71.8 g

Carbs: 10 g

Fiber:7 g

Protein: 3 g

78. Baked Mushrooms with Creamy Brussels Sprouts

Preparation Time: 8 Minutes

Cooking Time: 2 Hours 35 Minutes

Servings: 4

Ingredients:

For the mushrooms:

1 lb whole white button mushrooms

Salt and black pepper to taste

2 tsp dried thyme   1 bay leaf

5 black peppercorns

½ cups vegetable broth

2 garlic cloves, minced

1 ½ oz fresh ginger, grated

1 tbsp coconut oil   1 tbsp smoked paprika

For the creamy Brussel sprouts:

½ lb Brussel sprouts, halved

1 ½ cups cashew cream

Salt and ground black pepper to taste

Directions:

For the mushroom roast:

Preheat the oven to 200 F.

Pour all the mushroom ingredients into a baking dish, stir well, and cover with foil. Bake in the oven until softened, 1 to 2 hours.

Remove the dish, take off the foil, and use a slotted spoon to fetch the mushrooms onto serving plates. Set aside.

For the creamy Brussel sprouts:

Pour the broth in the baking dish into a medium pot and add the Brussel sprouts. Add about ½ cup of water if needed and cook for 7 to 10 minutes or until softened.

Stir in the cashew cream, adjust the taste with salt and black pepper, and simmer for 15 minutes.

Serve the creamy Brussel sprouts with the mushrooms.

Nutrition:

Calories: 492 Cal Fat: 37.9 g Carbs: 13 g

Fiber:2 g Protein: 29 g

79. Pimiento Tofu balls

Preparation Time: 10 Minutes

Cooking Time: 15 Minutes

Servings: 4

Ingredients: 1 tbsp Dijon mustard

¼ cup chopped pimientos

1/3 cup mayonnaise   3 tbsp cashew cream

1 tsp paprika powder

1 pinch cayenne pepper

4 oz grated vegan cheese

1 ½ lbs. tofu, pressed and crumbled

Salt and black pepper to taste

2 tbsp olive oil, for frying

Directions:

In a large bowl, add all the ingredients except for the olive oil and with gloves on your hands, mix the ingredients until well combined. Form bite size balls from the mixture.

Heat the olive oil in a medium non-stick skillet and fry the tofu balls in batches on both sides until brown and cooked through, 4 to 5 minutes on each side.

Transfer the tofu balls to a serving plate and serve warm.

Nutrition: Calories:254 Cal Fat: 36.8 g

Carbs: 12 g Fiber: 1 g Protein:26 g

80. Tempeh with Garlic Asparagus

Preparation Time: 10 Minutes

Cooking Time: 18 Minutes

Servings: 4

Ingredients:

For the tempeh:

3 tbsp vegan butter

4 tempeh slices

Salt and black pepper to taste

For the garlic buttered asparagus:

2 tbsp. olive oil

2 garlic cloves, minced

1 lb asparagus, trimmed and halved

Salt and black pepper to taste

1 tbsp dried parsley

1 small lemon, juiced

Directions:

For the tempeh:

Melt the vegan butter in a medium skillet over medium heat, season the tempeh with salt, black pepper and fry in the butter on both sides until brown and cooked through, 10 minutes. Transfer to a plate and set aside in a warmer for serving.

For the garlic asparagus:

Heat the olive oil in a medium skillet over medium heat, and sauté the garlic until fragrant, 30 seconds.

Stir in the asparagus, season with salt and black pepper, and cook until slightly softened with a bit of crunch, 5 minutes.

Mix in the parsley, lemon juice, toss to coat well, and plate the asparagus.

Serve the asparagus warm with the tempeh.

Nutrition:

Calories: 181

Fat:17.5 g

Carbs: 6 g

Fiber: 3 g

Protein: 3 g

81. Mushroom Curry Pie

Preparation Time: 15 Minutes

Cooking Time: 55 Minutes

Servings 4

Ingredients:

For the piecrust:

1 tbsp flax seed powder + 3 tbsp water

¾ cup coconut flour

4 tbsp chia seeds

4 tbsp almond flour

1 tbsp psyllium husk powder

1 tsp baking powder

1 pinch salt

3 tbsp olive oil

4 tbsp water

For the filling:

1 cup chopped cremini mushrooms

1 cup vegan mayonnaise

3 tbsp + 9 tbsp water

½ red bell pepper, finely chopped

1 tsp turmeric powder

½ tsp paprika powder

½ tsp garlic powder

¼ tsp black pepper

½ cup cashew cream

1¼ cups shredded tofu cheese

Directions:

In two separate bowls, mix the different portions of flax seed powder with the respective quantity of water and set aside to absorb for 5 minutes.

Preheat the oven to 350 F.

Make the crust:

When the flax egg is ready, pour the smaller quantity into a food processor, add the coconut flour, chia seeds, almond flour, psyllium husk powder, baking powder, salt, olive oil, and water. Blend the ingredients until a ball forms out of the dough.

Line a springform pan with an 8-inch diameter parchment paper and grease the pan with cooking spray.

Spread the dough in the bottom of the pan and bake in the oven for 15 minutes.

Make the filling:

In a bowl, add the remaining flax egg, mushrooms, mayonnaise, water, bell pepper, turmeric, paprika, garlic powder, black pepper, cashew cream, and tofu cheese. Combine the mixture evenly and fill the piecrust. Bake further for 40 minutes or until the pie is golden brown.

Remove, slice, and serve the pie with a chilled strawberry drink.

Nutrition:

Calories:548 Cal

Fat: 55.9 g

Carbs: 6 g

Fiber: 2 g

Protein: 8 g

82. Spicy Cheese with Tofu Balls

Preparation Time: 20 Minutes

Cooking Time: 20 Minutes

Servings: 4

Ingredients:

For the spicy cheese:

1/3 cup vegan mayonnaise

¼ cup pickled jalapenos

1 tsp paprika powder

1 tbsp mustard powder

1 pinch cayenne pepper

4 oz grated tofu cheese

For the tofu balls:

1 tbsp flax seed powder + 3 tbsp water

2 ½ cup crumbled tofu

Salt and black pepper

2 tbsp plant butter, for frying

Directions:

Make the spicy cheese. In a bowl, mix the mayonnaise, jalapenos, paprika, mustard powder, cayenne powder, and cheddar cheese. Set aside.

In another medium bowl, combine the flax seed powder with water and allow absorbing for 5 minutes.

Add the flax egg to the cheese mixture, the crumbled tofu, salt, and black pepper, and combine well. Use your hands to form large meatballs out of the mix.

Then, melt the vegan butter in a large skillet over medium heat and fry the tofu balls until cooked and browned on the outside.

Serve the tofu balls with roasted cauliflower mash and mayonnaise.

Nutrition:

Calories: 259 Cal

Fat: 55.9 g

Carbs: 5 g

Fiber: 1 g

Protein: 16 g

83. Tempeh Coconut Curry Bake

Preparation Time: 7minutes

Cooking Time: 23minutes

Servings: 4

Ingredients:

1 oz. plant butter, for greasing

2 ½ cups chopped tempeh

Salt and black pepper

4 tbsp plant butter

2 tbsp red curry paste

1 ½ cup coconut cream

½ cup fresh parsley, chopped

15 oz. cauliflower, cut into florets

Directions:

Preheat the oven to 400 F and grease a baking dish with 1 ounce of vegan butter.

Arrange the tempeh in the baking dish, sprinkle with salt and black pepper, and top each tempeh with a slice of the remaining butter.

In a bowl, mix the red curry paste with the coconut cream and parsley. Pour the mixture over the tempeh.

Bake in the oven for 20 minutes or until the tempeh is cooked.

While baking, season the cauliflower with salt, place in a microwave-safe bowl, and sprinkle with some water. Steam in the microwave for 3 minutes or until the cauliflower is soft and tender within.

Remove the curry bake and serve with the caulis.

Nutrition:

Calories:417 Cal

Fat:38.8 g Carbs: 11 g

Fiber: 2 g

Protein: 11 g

84. Kale and Mushroom Pierogis

Preparation Time:15 Minutes

Cooking Time: 30 Minutes

Servings: 4

Ingredients:

For the stuffing:

2 tbsp vegan butter

2 garlic cloves, finely chopped

1 small red onion, finely chopped

3 oz. baby bella mushrooms, sliced

2 oz. fresh kale

½ tsp salt   ¼ tsp black pepper

½ cup cashew cream   2 oz. grated tofu cheese

For the pierogi:

1 tbsp flax seed powder + 3 tbsp water

½ cup almond flour

4 tbsp coconut flour

½ tsp salt   1 tsp baking powder

1½ cups shredded tofu cheese

5 tbsp ve gan butter

Olive oil for brushing

Directions:

Put the vegan butter in a skillet and melt over medium heat, then add and sauté the garlic, red onion, mushrooms, and kale until the mushrooms brown.

Season the mixture with salt and black pepper and reduce the heat to low. Stir in the cashew cream and tofu cheese and simmer for 1 minute. Turn the heat off and set the filling aside to cool.

Make the pierogis: In a small bowl, mix the flax seed powder with water and allow sitting for 5 minutes.

In a bowl, combine the almond flour, coconut flour, salt, and baking powder.

Put a small pan over low heat, add, and melt the tofu cheese and vegan butter while stirring continuously until smooth batter forms. Turn the heat off.

Pour the flax egg into the cream mixture, continue stirring, while adding the flour mixture until a firm dough form.

Mold the dough into four balls, place on a chopping board, and use a rolling pin to flatten each into ½ inch thin round pieces.

Spread a generous amount of stuffing on one-half of each dough, then fold over the filling, and seal the dough with your fingers.

Brush with olive oil, place on a baking sheet, and bake for 20 minutes or until the pierogis turn a golden-brown color.

Serve the pierogis with a lettuce tomato salad.

Nutrition: Calories:364

Fat:33.4 g Carbs:8g Fiber:2g Protein:12 g

85. Mushroom Lettuce Wraps

Preparation Time: 5minutes

Cooking Time: 16minutes

Servings: 4

Ingredients: 2 tbsp vegan butter

4 oz. baby bella mushrooms, sliced

1½ lbs. tofu, crumbled

½ tsp salt   ¼ tsp black pepper

1 iceberg lettuce, leaves extracted

1 cup shredded vegan cheese

1 large tomato, sliced

Directions:

Put the vegan butter in a skillet and melt over medium heat. Add the mushrooms and sauté until browned and tender, about 6 minutes. Transfer the mushrooms to a plate and set aside.

Add the tofu to the skillet, season with salt and black pepper, and cook until brown, about 10 minutes. Turn the heat off.

Spoon the tofu and mushrooms into the lettuce leaves, sprinkle with the vegan cheese, and share the tomato slices on top.

Serve the burger immediately.

Nutrition:

Calories:439 Cal Fat:31.9 g

Carbs: 9 g Fiber: 4 g Protein: 36 g

86. Tofu and Spinach Lasagna with Red Sauce

Preparation Time: 20 Minutes

Cooking Time: 45 Minutes

Servings: 4

Ingredients:

2 tbsp vegan butter

1 white onion, chopped

1 garlic clove, minced

2 ½ cups crumbled tofu

3 tbsp tomato paste

½ tbsp dried oregano

1 tsp salt

¼ tsp ground black pepper

½ cup water

1 cup baby spinach

Keto pasta

Flax egg: 8 tbsp flax seed powder + 1 ½ cups water

1 ½ cup dairy-free cashew cream

1 tsp salt

5 tbsp psyllium husk powder

Dairy-free cheese topping

2 cups coconut cream

5 oz. shredded vegan mozzarella cheese

2 oz. grated tofu cheese

½ tsp salt

¼ tsp ground black pepper

½ cup fresh parsley, finely chopped

Directions:

Melt the vegan butter in a medium pot over medium heat. Then, add the white onion and garlic, and sauté until fragrant and soft, about 3 minutes.

Stir in the tofu and cook until brown. Mix in the tomato paste, oregano, salt, and black pepper.

Pour the water into the pot, stir, and simmer the ingredients until most of the liquid has evaporated.

While cooking the sauce, make the lasagna sheets. Preheat the oven to 300 F and mix the flax seed powder with the water in a medium bowl to make flax egg. Allow sitting to thicken for 5 minutes.

Combine the flax egg with the cashew cream and salt. Add the psyllium husk powder a bit at a time while whisking and allow the mixture to sit for a few more minutes.

Line a baking sheet with parchment paper and spread the mixture in. Cover with another parchment paper and use a rolling pin to flatten the dough into the sheet.

Bake the batter in the oven for 10 to 12 minutes, remove after, take off the parchment

papers, and slice the pasta into sheets that fit your baking dish.

In a bowl, combine the coconut cream and two-thirds of the mozzarella cheese. Fetch out 2 tablespoons of the mixture and reserve.

Mix in the tofu cheese, salt, black pepper, and parsley. Set aside.

Grease your baking dish with cooking spray, layer a single line of pasta in the dish, spread with some tomato sauce, 1/3 of the spinach, and ¼ of the coconut cream mixture. Season with salt and black pepper as desired.

Repeat layering the ingredients twice in the same manner making sure to top the final layer with the coconut cream mixture and the reserved cashew cream.

Bake in the oven for 30 minutes at 400 F or until the lasagna has a beautiful brown surface.

Remove the dish; allow cooling for a few minutes, and slice.

Serve the lasagna with a baby green salad.

Nutrition:

Calories:767 Cal

Fat: 69.8 g

Carbs:14g

Fiber: 3g

Protein: 28 g

87. Green Avocado Carbonara

Preparation Time: 15 Minutes

Cooking Time: 15 Minutes

Servings: 4

Ingredients:

8 tbsp flax seed powder + 1 ½ cups water

1 ½ cups dairy-free cashew cream

1 tsp salt

5 ½ tbsp psyllium husk powder

Avocado sauce

1 avocado, peeled and pitted

1 ¾ cups coconut cream

Juice of ½ lemon

1 teaspoon onion powder

½ teaspoon garlic powder

¼ cup olive oil

¾ teaspoon sea salt

¼ teaspoon black pepper

Walnut Parmesan or store-bought parmesan

For serving

4 tbsp toasted pecans

½ cup freshly grated tofu cheese

Directions:

Preheat the oven to 300 F.

In a medium bowl, mix the flax seed powder with water and allow sitting to thicken for 5 minutes.

Add the cashew cream, salt, and psyllium husk powder. Whisk until smooth batter forms.

Line a baking sheet with parchment paper, pour in the batter and cover with another parchment paper. Use a rolling pin to flatten the dough into the sheet.

Place in the oven and bake for 10 to 12 minutes. Remove the pasta after, take off the parchment papers and use a sharp knife to slice the pasta into thin strips lengthwise. Cut each piece into halves, pour into a bowl, and set aside.

For the avocado sauce, in a blender, combine the avocado, coconut cream, lemon juice, onion powder, and garlic powder. Puree the ingredients until smooth.

Pour the olive oil over the pasta and stir to coat properly. Pour the avocado sauce on top and mix. Then, season with salt, black pepper, and the soy cheese. Combine again.

Divide the pasta into serving plates, garnish with extra soy cheese and pecans, and serve immediately.

Nutrition:

Calories:941 Fat:94.2 g

Carbs:19 g Fiber:8 g

Protein:16g

88. Cashew Buttered Quesadillas with Leafy Greens

Preparation Time: 10 Minutes

Cooking Time: 20 Minutes

Servings: 4

Ingredients:

Tortillas

3 tbsp flax seed powder + ½ cup water

½ cup dairy-free cashew cream

1½ tsp psyllium husk powder

1 tbsp coconut flour

½ tsp salt

Filling

1 tbsp cashew butter, for frying

5 oz. grated vegan cheese

1 oz. leafy greens

Directions:

Preheat the oven to 400 F.

In a bowl, mix the flax seed powder with water and allow sitting to thicken for 5 minutes.

After, whisk the cashew cream into the flax egg until the batter is smooth.

In another bowl, combine the psyllium husk powder, coconut flour, and salt. Add the flour mixture to the flax egg batter and fold in until

fully incorporated. Allow sitting for a few minutes.

Then, line a baking sheet with parchment paper and pour in the mixture. Spread into the baking sheet using a spatula and bake in the upper rack of the oven for 5 to 7 minutes or until brown around the edges. Keep a watchful eye on the tortillas to prevent burning.

Remove when ready and slice into 8 pieces. Set aside.

For the filling, spoon a little cashew butter into a skillet and place a tortilla in the pan. Sprinkle with some vegan cheese, leafy greens, and cover with another tortilla.

Brown each side of the quesadilla for 1 minute or until the cheese melts. Transfer to a plate.

Repeat assembling the quesadillas using the remaining cashew butter.

Serve immediately with avocado salad.

Nutrition:

Calories: 224 Cal

Fat: 20.4 g

Carbs: 1 g

Fiber: 0g

Protein: 9 g

89. Zucchini Boats with Vegan Cheese

Preparation Time: 3 Minutes

Cooking Time: 4 Minutes

Servings: 2

Ingredients:

1 medium-sized zucchini

4 tbsp vegan butter

2 garlic cloves, minced

1½ oz. baby kale

Salt and black pepper to taste

2 tbsp unsweetened tomato sauce

1 cup vegan cheese

Olive oil for drizzling

Directions:

Preheat the oven to 375 F.

Use a knife to slice the zucchini in halves and scoop out the pulp with a spoon into a plate. Keep the flesh.

Grease a baking sheet with cooking spray and place the zucchini boats on top.

Put the vegan butter in a skillet and melt over medium heat. Add and sauté the garlic until fragrant and slightly browned, about 4 minutes.

Add the kale and the zucchini pulp. Cook until the kale wilts; season with salt and black pepper.

Spoon the tomato sauce into the boats and spread to coat the bottom evenly. Then, spoon the kale mixture into the zucchinis and sprinkle with the cheese.

Bake in the oven for 20 to 25 minutes or until the cheese has a beautiful golden color.

Plate the zucchinis when ready, drizzle with olive oil, and season with salt and black pepper.

Serve immediately.

Nutrition:

Calories: 721 Cal Fat: 76.8 g

Carbs: 2 g Fiber: 0 g Protein: 9 g

90. Tempeh Garam Masala Bake

Preparation Time: 5 Minutes

Cooking Time: 24 Minutes

Servings: 4

Ingredients:

3 tbsp vegan butter

3 cups tempeh slices

Salt

2 tbsp garam masala

1 green bell pepper, finely diced

1¼ cups coconut cream

1 tbsp fresh cilantro, finely chopped

Directions:

Preheat the oven to 400 F.

Place a skillet over medium heat, add, and melt the vegan butter. Meanwhile, season the tempeh with some salt. Fry the tempeh in the butter until browned on both sides, about 4 minutes.

Stir half of the garam masala into the tempeh until evenly mixed; turn the heat off.

Transfer the tempeh with the spice into a baking dish.

Then, in a small bowl, mix the green bell pepper, coconut cream, cilantro, and remaining garam masala.

Pour the mixture over the tempeh and bake in the oven for 20 minutes or until golden brown on top.

Garnish with cilantro and serve with some cauli rice.

Nutrition:

Calories:286 Cal

Fat: 27 g

Carbs: 5 g

Fibe r: 0 g

Protein:9 g

91. Caprese Casserole

Preparation Time: 5 Minutes

Cooking Time: 20 Minutes

Servings: 4

Ingredients: 1 cup cherry tomatoes, halved

1 cup vegan mozzarella cheese, cut into small pieces

2 tbsp basil pesto

1 cup vegan mayonnaise

2 oz. tofu cheese

Salt and black pepper

1 cup arugula

4 tbsp olive oil

Directions:

Preheat the oven to 350 F.

In a baking dish, mix the cherry tomatoes, mozzarella, basil pesto, mayonnaise, half of the tofu cheese, salt, and black pepper.

Level the ingredients with a spatula and sprinkle the remaining tofu cheese on top. Bake for 20 minutes or until the top of the casserole is golden brown.

Remove and allow cooling for a few minutes. Slice and dish into plates, top with some arugula and drizzle with olive oil. Serve.

Nutrition: Calories: 588 Cal Fat: 59 g

Carbs: 2 g Fiber: 1 g Protein: 13 g

92. Lemon Garlic Mushrooms

Preparation Time: 25 Minutes

Cooking Time: 10 Minutes

Servings: 4

Ingredients: 3 oz enoki mushrooms

1 tbsp olive oil 1 tsp lemon zest, chopped

2 tbsp lemon juice

3 garlic cloves, sliced

6 oyster mushrooms, halved

5 oz cremini mushrooms, sliced

1/2 red chili, sliced

1 /2 onion, sliced

1 tsp sea salt

Directions:

Heat olive oil in a pan over high heat.

Add shallots, enoki mushrooms, oyster mushrooms, cremini mushrooms, and chili.

Stir well and cook over medium-high heat for 10 minutes.

Add lemon zest and stir well. Season with lemon juice and salt and cook for 3-4 minutes.

Serve and enjoy.

Nutrition:

Calories: 87 Cal Fat: 5.6 gCarbs: 7.5 g

Sugar: 1.8 g Protein: 3 g

93. Almond Green Beans

Preparation Time: 20 Minutes

Cooking Time: 5 Minutes

Servings: 4

Ingredients: ½ tsp sea salt

1 lb fresh green beans, trimmed

1/3 cup almonds, sliced 4 garlic cloves, sliced

2 tbsp olive oil 1 tbsp lemon juice

Directions:

Add green beans, salt, and lemon juice in a mixing bowl. Toss well and set aside. Heat oil in a pan over medium heat. Add sliced almonds and sauté until lightly browned. Add garlic and sauté for 30 seconds.

Pour almond mixture over green beans and toss well.

Stir well and serve immediately.

Nutrition: Calories: 146 Cal Fat: 11.2 g Carbs: 10.9 g Sugar: 2 g Protein: 4 g

94. Fried Okra

Preparation Time: 20 Minutes

Cooking Time: 5 Minutes

Servings: 4

Ingredients:

1 lb fresh okra, cut into ¼" slices

1/3 cup almond meal

Pepper

Salt

Oil for frying

Directions:

Heat oil in large pan over medium-high heat.

In a bowl, mix together sliced okra, almond meal, pepper, and salt until well coated.

Once the oil is hot then add okra to the hot oil and cook until lightly browned.

Remove fried okra from pan and allow to drain on paper towels.

Serve and enjoy.

Nutrition:

Calories: 91 Cal

Fat: 4.2 g

Carbs: 10.2 g

Sugar: 10.2 g

Protein: 3.9 g

95. Super Healthy Beet Greens Salad

Preparation Time: 10 Minutes

Cooking Time: 0

Servings: 4

Ingredients:

For Dressing:

1 garlic clove, minced

1 ½ teaspoons of dijon mustard

3 tablespoons of extra-virgin olive oil

1 tablespoon balsamic vinegar

Salt and freshly ground black pepper, to taste

2 cups of vegetable broth ¼ cup of olive oil

For Salad:

8 cup of fresh beet greens

¼ cup of feta cheese, crumbled

Directions:

Prepare dressing in a bowl by adding all the dressing ingredients and beat until well combined. In a large bowl, mix together greens and cheese.

Pour dressing over salad and toss to coat well. Serve immediately.

Nutrition:

Calories: 280   Fats: 26.2g   Carbs: 9.1g

Protein: 5.5g   Fiber: 3.6g

96. Coconut Yogurt with Chia Seeds and Almonds

Preparation Time: 10 Minutes

Cooking Time: 0

Servings: 4

Ingredients:

For Dressing:

1 1/3 cups of coconut yogurt

1 cup of unsweetened almond milk

8-10 drops of liquid stevia

Pinch of salt

1/3 cup of chia seeds

3 tablespoons of almonds, chopped

Directions:

In a bowl, add yogurt, milk, stevia, and salt and beat until well combined.

Add chia seeds and beat until well combined.

Refrigerate, covered for at least 4 hours.

Serve with a sprinkle of chopped almonds.

Nutrition:

Calories: 182 Cal

Fats: 9.1g

Carbs: 14.4g

Protein: 4.7g

Fiber: 10.8g

97. Super Delicious Cucumber Salad

Preparation Time: 10 Minutes

Cooking Time: 0

Servings: 8

Ingredients:

½ cup of sour cream

1 teaspoon of white vinegar

½ teaspoon of powdered stevia

½ teaspoon of dill weed

Salt, to taste

4 medium cucumbers, sliced

Directions:

In a bowl, add all the ingredients except cucumbers and beat until well combined.

Add cucumber slices and stir until well combined.

Refrigerate to chill for at least 30 minutes before serving.

Nutrition:

Calories: 54 Cal

Fats: 3.2g

Carbs: 6.1g

Protein: 1.4g

Fiber: 0.8g

98. Pudding Delight with Banana & Coconut

Preparation Time: 15 Minutes

Cooking Time: 0

Servings: 4

Ingredients:

1 medium banana, peeled and quartered

2 tablespoons of unsweetened coconut milk

1 packet of stevia

1 teaspoon of vanilla extract

1 cup of plain Greek yogurt

2 tablespoons of unsweetened coconut, shredded

Directions:

In a blender, add quartered bananas, milk, stevia, and vanilla extract and beat until well combined and smooth.

Transfer the mixture into a bowl.

Gently, fold in yogurt.

Refrigerate to chill completely.

Garnish with coconut and serve.

Nutrition:

Calories: 103 Cal Fats: 4g

Carbs: 10.2g   Protein: 6.9g

Fiber: 1.2g

99. Extra Easy Cheese Sandwich

Preparation Time: 15 Minutes

Cooking Time: 5 Mins

Servings: 1

Ingredients:

2 tablespoons of almond flour

2 tablespoons of butter, softened

1½ tablespoons of psyllium husk powder

½ teaspoon of baking powder

2 large organic eggs

For Sandwiches:

2 tablespoons of cheddar cheese, grated

1 tablespoon of butter

Directions:

In a bowl, add all the bun ingredients except eggs and mix until a dough forms.

Add eggs and mix until a thick dough form.

Press each dough in a microwave safe square container.

Smooth the surface and clean of the sides.

Microwave for about 90-100 seconds.

Remove from microwave and keep aside to cool slightly.

Carefully remove the bun from container.

Cut the bun in half.

Place the cheese over cut side of 1 bun slices.

Cover with remaining bun slice to make a sandwich.

In a skillet, melt butter on medium heat.

Add sandwich and cook for about 1-2 minutes per side.

Nutrition:

Calories: 577 Cal F ats: 55.1g

Carbs: 4.7g Protein: 19g

Fiber: 1.6g

100. India Super Easy Summer Cooler

Preparation Time: 5 Minutes

Cooking Time: 0

Servings: 2

Ingredients:

1 cup of plain greek yogurt

1 cup of chilled water

Pinch of ground cumin

Pinch of paprika

Pinch of salt

Directions:

In a bowl, add yogurt and beat until smooth.

Slowly, add water, beating continuously.

Add spices and stir to combine well.

Pour into 2 serving glasses and serve immediately.

Nutrition:

Calories: 48 Cal

Fats: 1.3g

Carbs: 2.6g

Protein: 6.3g

Fiber: 0g

Dessert Recipes

101. Strawberry Coconut Parfait

Preparation Time: 5 Minutes

Cooking Time: 0

Servings: 4

Ingredients:

2 cups cold coconut yogurt

¼ cup fresh strawberries

½ lemon, zested

8 mint leaves

2 tbsp chia seeds

Maple (sugar-free) syrup to taste

Directions:

In four medium serving glasses, layer half of coconut yogurt, strawberries, lemon zest, mint leaves, chia seeds, and drizzle with maple syrup. Repeat with a second layer.

Serve.

Nutrition: Calories: 105 Cal

Fat: 7.82 g Carbs: 4.5 g

Fiber: 1.58 g

Protein: 5.24 g

102. Lemon-Chocolate Truffles

Preparation Time: 5 Minutes

Cooking Time: 30 Minutes

Servings: 4

Ingredients: 2/3 cup heavy cream

2/3 cup unsweetened dark chocolate, roughly chopped

½ lemon, juiced

¼ cup unsweetened cocoa powder

2 tbsp swerve sugar

Directions:

Over low fire, heat heavy cream in a small saucepan until tiny bubbles form around edges of pan. Turn heat off.

Add dark chocolate, swirl pan to coat chocolate with cream, and gently stir mixture until smooth.

Mix in lemon juice, pour mixture into a bowl, and chill for 4 hours or until mixture hardens for molding.

Line two baking trays with parchment papers; set one aside and mix cocoa powder and swerve sugar in other.

Remove chocolate mixture from fridge; form bite-size balls and coat in cocoa powder.

Place truffles on other baking tray and chill for 30 minutes before serving.

Nutrition:

Calories: 143 Cal Fat: 12.68 g

Carbs: 3.13 g Fiber: 2.5 g Protein: 2.41 g

103. Blackberry and Red Wine Crumble

Preparation Time: 10 Minutes

Cooking Time: 45 Minutes

Servings: 6

Ingredients:

2 cups blackberries

¼ cup red wine

1 tsp cinnamon powder

1 tsp vanilla extract

1 ¼ cup erythritol, divided

1 cup cold salted butter, cubed

¾ cup coconut flour

1 ½ cups almond flour

Directions:

Preheat oven to 375o F.

In a baking dish, add blackberries, red wine, cinnamon powder, vanilla, half of erythritol, and stir.

In a medium bowl, using your hands, rub butter with coconut flour, almond flour, and remaining erythritol until resembles large breadcrumbs.

Spread mixture over blackberries making sure to cover well; bake until golden brown on top, 45 minutes.

Remove from oven; allow cooling for 3 minutes and serve warm.

Nutrition:

Calories: 318 Cal

Fat: 31.34 g

Carbs: 9.79 g

Fiber: 4.9 g

Protein: 1.5 g

104. Cinnamon-Chocolate Cake

Preparation Time: 20 Minutes

Cooking Time: 45 Minutes

Servings: 4

Ingredients: ½ cup melted butter

1 cup almond flour

½ cup unsweetened dark chocolate, melted

1 cup erythritol 2 tsp vanilla caviar

½ tsp salt 2 tsp cinnamon powder

½ cup boiling water 3 large eggs

Swerve confectioner's sugar for garnishing

Directions:

Preheat oven to 350oF, lightly grease a springform pan with cooking spray and line with parchment paper. Set aside.

In a large bowl, mix butter, almond flour, chocolate, erythritol, vanilla, salt, cinnamon powder, and boiling water. Crack eggs one after another while continually beating until smooth. Pour batter into springform pan and bake in oven until a toothpick inserted comes out clean, 45 minutes.

Remove from oven; allow cooling in pan for 10 minutes and turn over onto a wire rack.

Dust with swerve confectioner's sugar, slice, and serve.

Nutrition: Calories: 417 Cal Fat: 41.75 g

Carbs: 11.53 g Fiber: 9.8 g Protein: 16.45 g

105. Himalayan Raspberry Fat Bombs

Preparation Time: 15 Minutes

Cooking Time: 0

Servings: 4

Ingredients:

3 cups golden Himalayan raspberries

1 tsp vanilla extract

16 oz cream cheese, room temperature

4 tbsp unsalted butter

2 tbsp maple (sugar-free) syrup

Directions:

Line a 12-holed muffin tray with cake liners and set aside.

Pour raspberries, vanilla into a blender, and puree until smooth.

In a small saucepan, over medium heat, melt cream cheese and butter until well-combined.

In a medium bowl, evenly combine raspberry mix, cream cheese mix, and maple syrup. Pour mixture into muffin holes.

Refrigerate for 40 minutes and serve after.

Nutrition:

Calories: 227 g Fat: 14.8 g

Carbs: 5.2 g Fiber: 2.1 g Protein: 4.68 g

106. Cashew-Chocolate Cheesecake

Preparation Time: 10 Minutes

Cooking Time: 6 Minutes

Servings: 4

Ingredients:

For crust:

1 cup raw cashew nuts

½ cup salted butter, melted

2 tbsp swerve sugar

For cake:

1 tsp agar powder

2 tbsp lemon juice

2/3 cup unsweetened dark chocolate, chopped + extra for garnishing

4 tbsp unsalted butter, melted

1 ½ cups cream cheese

½ cup erythritol

1 cup Greek yogurt

Directions:

For crust:

Preheat oven to 350oF.

In a food processor, blend cashews until finely ground. Add butter, swerve sugar, and mix until combined.

Press crust mixture firmly into bottom of a spring form pan.

Bake for 5 minutes and chill while you prepare the filling.

For cake:

In a small pot, combine agar with lemon juice, and a tablespoon of water. Allow sitting for 5 minutes and then, set pot over medium heat to dissolve agar. Set aside.

In a medium safe-microwave bowl, add dark chocolate, butter, and microwave for 1 minute to melt, stirring at every 10 seconds interval. Set aside.

In another medium bowl, beat cream cheese with erythritol until smooth. Stir in agar and yogurt until evenly combined. Fold in chocolate and mix well.

Remove pan from fridge and pour cream mixture on top. Tap sides of pan gently to release trapped air bubbles; transfer pan to fridge and chill for at least 3 hours.

When ready, remove and release cake from pan, garnish with dark chocolate, and slice.

Serve immediately.

Nutrition:

Calories: 235 Cal

Fat: 14.12 g

Carbs: 7.3 g

Fiber: 3.5 g Protein: 6.78 g

107. Creamy Avocado Drink

Preparation Time: 5 Minutes

Cooking Time: 0

Servings: 4

Ingredients:

4 large ripe avocados, halved and pitted

1 tsp vanilla extract

4 tbsp erythritol

¼ cup cold unsweetened almond milk

1 tbsp cold heavy cream

Directions:

In a blender, add avocado pulp, vanilla extract, erythritol, almond milk, and heavy cream. Process until smooth.

Pour mixture into serving glasses and serve immediately.

Nutrition:

Calories: 388 Cal

Fat: 32.16 g

Carbs: 5.42 g

Fiber: 3.32 g

Protein: 6.95 g

108. Raspberry Cookies

Preparation Time: 10 Minutes

Cooking Time: 25 Minutes

Servings: 6

Ingredients: 1 tablespoon ground flaxseed

1 cup blanched almond flour

2 tablespoon coconut flour

1 cup granulated Swerve

1/2 cup almond butter

1/8 teaspoon vanilla extract

1/4 cup almond milk 1/2 cup raspberries

1/4 cup sugar-free chocolate chips

Directions: Mix ground flaxseed with 2.5 tablespoon water in a bowl and keep it aside for 10 minutes. Let your oven preheat at 350 degrees F then layer an 8-inch pan with parchment paper. IN a bowl whisk all the dry ingredients then stir in almond butter, milk, vanilla extracts, and flaxseed mixture. Mix well until combined, add few drops of more milk if the mixture is too thick. Fold in half of the chocolate and raspberries to the batter. Spread this raspberry batter in the layered pan evenly then top it with remaining raspberries and chocolate chips. Bake the batter for 25 minutes until golden brown. Slice and serve fresh.

Nutrition: Calories: 234 Cal

Fat: 17.3 g Carbs: 6.9 g Protein: 4.8 g

109. Lenny & Larry's Cookies

Preparation Time: 10 Minutes

Cooking Time: 10 Minutes

Servings: 6

Ingredients:

3 tablespoon coconut flour

1 scoop vanilla protein powder

2 tablespoon nut butter

1 tablespoon swerve

1-2 tablespoon almond milk

Directions:

Let your oven preheat at 350 degrees F and layer a baking tray with parchment paper.

Whisk everything dry in a bowl first then stir in wet ingredients.

Mix well until it forms crumbly mixture then add some liquid to make a thick batter.

Make small dough balls out of this mixture and place them in the baking tray.

Press the balls with the palm of your hand to make flat cookies.

Bake them for 10 minutes then serve.

Nutrition:

Calories: 206 Cal

Fat: 20.3 g Carbs: 2.6 g

Protein: 4.2 g

110. Zucchini Chocolate Brownies

Preparation Time: 10 Minutes

Cooking Time: 25 Minutes

Servings: 6

Ingredients: 1/3 cup coconut oil

1 1/4 cups chocolate chips

3/4 cup granulated Swerve

1/4 cup zucchini, grated   2 large eggs

2 tablespoon cocoa powder

3 tablespoon arrowroot powder

Directions:

Let your oven preheat at 350 degrees F. Layer an 8-inch pan with parchment sheet and grease it with cooking oil.

Melt and mix chocolate with coconut oil in a bowl by heating in the microwave for 30 seconds.Whisk this mixture with eggs, sweetener, and zucchini. Stir in arrowroot powder and cocoa powder. Mix well until smooth.

Spread this mixture in the pan evenly then bake it for 25 minutes until done. Allow it to cool for 15 minutes then slice.

Enjoy fresh.

Nutrition:

Calories: 280 Cal Fat: 23 g

Carbs: 3.1 g Protein: 3.9 g

111. Fudgy Pumpkin Brownies

Preparation Time: 10 Minutes

Cooking Time: 35 Minutes

Servings: 4

Ingredients: 4 eggs

1 cup pumpkin puree 1 cup mashed avocado

2 cups of cocoa powder

6 tablespoon coconut flour

2/3 cup swerve

1 tablespoon baking soda

1 cup unsweetened coconut milk

1/2 cup sugar-free chocolate chips

Directions:

Let your oven preheat at 350 degrees F. Layer an 8-inch pan with parchment paper. On high speed blend everything in a food processor except chocolate chips and coconut milk. Once mix well then add ½ cup coconut milk and continue mixing. Add more coconut milk if the mixture is too thick. Spread this batter evenly in the layered pan and sprinkle chocolate chips over the batter. Bake the batter for 35 minutes until golden brown.

Slice and serve fresh.

Nutrition:

Calories: 211 Cal Fat: 26 g

Carbs: 3.1 g Protein: 3.9 g

112. Cinnamon Roll Bars

Preparation Time: 10 Minutes

Cooking Time: 0

Servings: 6

Ingredients: 3/4 cup coconut flour

2 cups cashew butter   1/2 cup swerve

1 1/2 tablespoon cinnamon divided

8 oz cream cheese, softened

1/4 cup granulated Swerve

Directions:

Layer an 8-inch pan with parchment paper then keep it aside.

Mix smooth nut butter, coconut flour and a tablespoon of cinnamon in a bowl to make a thick batter.

Add some more liquid if the mixture is too thick then transfer this mixture to a pan.

Spread this mixture evenly and refrigerate for a few hours.

Meanwhile, beat cream cheese with sweetener and half tablespoon cinnamon.

Spread this mixture over the refrigerate batter evenly. Slice the base into 12 equal-sized bars.

Serve fresh.

Nutrition:

Calories: 166 Cal Fat : 25.5 g Carbs: 5.5 g

Protein: 4.9 g

113.   Snickers Bars

Preparation Time: 10 Minutes

Cooking Time: 1 Minute

Servings: 6

Ingredients: 1.5 cups almond butter

1 cup salted nuts   1/2 cup nut or seed butter

3/4 cup coconut flour

2 cups almond butter 1/2 cup swerve

1 teaspoon water 1-2 tablespoon almond milk

1-2 cups sugar-free chocolate chips

Directions:

Blend almond butter with nuts in a food processor on high speed to make a thick paste.

Spread this mixture in an 8-inch pan, lined with parchment paper and refrigerate.

Prepare the caramel by heating seed butter, coconut oil, and swerve in a pan.

Pour this mixture in the pan and freeze again until firm. Slice the base into small-sized bars.

Melt chocolate in a bowl by heating in the microwave for a 1 minute. Dip the bars in the melted chocolate and refrigerate them until chocolate is set. Enjoy fresh.

Nutrition:

Calories: 181 Cal Fat: 14.7 g

Carbs: 7.4 g Protein: 6.3 g

114.   Lemon Coconut Crack Bars

Preparation Time: 10 Minutes

Cooking Time: 0

Servings: 6

Ingredients:

3 cups unsweetened shredded coconut

1-2 tablespoon lemon rind, chopped

1/3 cup coconut oil

3/4 cup swerve

Directions:

Toss everything into a large mixing bowl and mix well until combined.

Layer an 8-inch pan with parchment paper.

Spread the prepared batter in the pan evenly and firmly.

Place the pan in the freezer then slice the batter into small bars.

Enjoy fresh.

Nutrition:

Calories: 149 Cal

Fat: 15.1 g

Carbs: 5.1 g

Protein: 0.8 g

115. Gingerbread Cookie Bars

Preparation Time: 10 Minutes

Cooking Time:

Servings: 6

Ingredients: 2 cups cashew butter

1/2 cup swerve 3/4 cup coconut flour

1 teaspoon nutmeg 2 teaspoon ground ginger

1 teaspoon cinnamon

1 serving cream cheese

Directions:

Melt and mix cashew butter with sweetener in a bowl by heating in the microwave for 30 seconds.

Start adding the remaining ingredients and mix well to form a thick batter.

Layer an 8-inch square pan with parchment paper.

Spread the prepared batter in the pan evenly and firmly. Refrigerate for 4 hours.

Slice into small bars and top them with cream cheese.

Refrigerate again for 30 minutes.

Enjoy.

Nutrition:

Calories: 103 Cal Fat: 12.3 g

Carbs: 8.4 g Protein: 3.1g

116. Cocoa Berries Mousse

Preparation Time: 10 Minutes

Cooking Time: 0

Servings: 2

Ingredients:

1 tablespoon cocoa powder

1 cup blackberries

1 cup blueberries

¾ cup coconut cream

1 tablespoon stevia

Directions:

In a blender, combine the berries with the cocoa and the other ingredients, pulse well, divide into bowls and keep in the fridge for 2 hours before serving.

Nutrition:

Calories: 200 Cal

Fat: 8 g

Fiber: 3.4 g

Carbs: 7.6 g

Protein: 4.3 g

117.   Nutmeg Pudding

Preparation Time: 10 Minutes

Cooking Time: 20 Minutes

Servings: 6

Ingredients:

2 tablespoons stevia

1 teaspoon nutmeg, ground

1 cup cauliflower rice

2 tablespoons flaxseed mixed with 3 tablespoons water

2 cups almond milk

¼ teaspoon nutmeg, grated

Directions:

In a pan, combine the cauliflower rice with the flaxseed mix and the other ingredients, whisk, cook over medium heat for 20 minutes, divide into bowls and serve cold.

Nutrition:

Calories: 220 Cal

Fat: 6.6 g

Fib er: 3.4 g

Carbs: 12.4 g

Protein: 3.4 g

118.   Lime Cherries and Rice Pudding

Preparation Time: 10 Minutes

Cooking Time: 25 Minutes

Servings: 4

Ingredients:

¾ cup stevia

2 cups coconut milk

3 tablespoons flaxseed mixed with 4 tablespoons water

Juice of 2 limes

Zest of 1 lime, grated

1 cup cherries, pitted and halved

1 cup cauliflower rice

Directions:

In a pan, combine the milk with the stevia and bring to a simmer over medium heat.

Add the cauliflower rice and the other ingredients, stir, cook for 25 minutes more, divide into cups and serve cold.

Nutrition:

Calories: 199 Cal

Fat: 5.4 g

Fiber: 3.4 g Carbs: 11g

Protein: 5.6 g

119. Chocolate Pudding

Preparation Time: 10 Minutes

Cooking Time: 20 Minutes

Servings: 4

Ingredients: 2 tablespoons cocoa powder

2 tablespoons coconut oil, melted

2/3 cup coconut cream

2 tablespoons stevia

¼ teaspoon almond extract

Directions:

In a pan, combine the cocoa powder with the coconut milk and the other ingredients, whisk, bring to a simmer ad cook over medium heat for 20 minutes.

Divide into cups and serve cold.

Nutrition:

Calories: 134 Cal Fat: 14.1 g

Fiber: 0.8 g Carbs: 3.1 g

Protein: 0.9 g

120. Coffee and Rhubarb Cream

Preparation Time: 10 Minutes

Cooking Time: 20 Minutes

Servings: 4

Ingredients:

¼ cup brewed coffee

2 tablespoons stevia

2 cups coconut cream

1 teaspoon vanilla extract

2 tablespoons coconut oil, melted

1 cup rhubarb, chopped

2 tablespoons flaxseed mixed with 3 tablespoons water

Directions:

In a bowl, mix the coffee with stevia, cream and the other ingredients, whisk well and divide into 4 ramekins.

Introduce the ramekins in the oven at 350 degrees F, bake for 20 minutes and serve warm.

Nutrition:

Calories: 300 Cal

Fat: 30.8 g

Fiber: 0 g

Carbs: 3 g

Protein: 4 g

121.   Chocolate Sea Salt Almonds

Preparation Time: 10 Minutes

Cooking Time: 0

Servings: 8

Ingredients:

4 ounces low-carb chocolate, chopped

1 tablespoon coconut oil

1 cup dry-roasted almonds

Sea salt

Directions:

Line a rimmed baking sheet with parchment paper.

In a small saucepan over medium-low heat, melt the chocolate and coconut oil together while stirring constantly. Remove from the heat once melted and pour into a small bowl.

Add the almonds to the chocolate and give them a good stir.

Using a teaspoon, remove a cluster of almonds and place it on the prepared baking sheet. Immediately sprinkle with a bit of sea salt.

Repeat step 4 with the remaining nuts.

Place the baking sheet in the refrigerator for 30 minutes or until set.

Remove and store the clusters in small resealable plastic bags (or cover each cluster with plastic wrap) in the refrigerator until ready to eat.

Nutrition:

Calories: 187 Cal Fat: 15 g

Protein: 6 g Carbs: 7 g Fiber: 4 g

122.   Salted Caramel Cashew Brittle

Preparation Time: 10 Minutes

Cook Time: 5 Minutes

Servings: 6

Ingredients:

8 tablespoons grass-fed butter

4 tablespoons brown erythritol, granulated

4 ounces raw unsalted cashews

4 tablespoons natural cashew butter

Coarse sea salt

Directions:

Line a rimmed baking sheet with parchment paper.

In a small saucepan over low heat, stir the butter until it melts.

Add the erythritol, cashews, and cashew butter. Mix until thoroughly combined and melted.

Pour the mixture onto the prepared baking sheet.

Sprinkle salt on top.

Place the baking sheet in the refrigerator to harden for about 1 hour.

Remove the brittle from the sheet and break into about 12 pieces.

Nutrition:

Calories: 321 Cal Fat: 29 g

Protein: 5 g Carbs: 10 gFiber: 1 g

123.   Cookies and Cream Parfait

Preparation Time: 5 Minutes

Cooking Time: 0

Servings: 1

Ingredients:

½ scoop low-carb vanilla protein powder

¾ cup plain full-fat Greek yogurt

1 Oreo cookie

4 tablespoons sugar-free chocolate syrup (I like Walden Farms)

Directions:

In a small bowl, mix together the protein powder and Greek yogurt until smooth and creamy.

Remove one side of the Oreo cookie. Place it in a small resealable plastic bag and crush it with the back of a spoon. Set aside.

Pour the chocolate syrup over the yogurt mixture and sprinkle with the cookie crumbles.

Nutrition:

Calories: 281 Cal Fat: 13 g Protein: 19 g

Carbs: 22 g Fiber: 3 g

124.   Pecan Pie Pudding

Preparation Time: 5 Minutes

Cooking Time: 0

Servings: 1

Ingredients:

¾ cup plain full-fat Greek yogurt

½ scoop low-carb vanilla protein powder

4 tablespoons chopped pecans

2 tablespoons sugar-free syrup

Directions:

In a small bowl, mix together the Greek yogurt and protein powder until smooth and creamy.

Top with the chopped pecans and syrup.

Nutrition: Calories: 381 Cal Fat: 21 g

Protein: 32 gCarbs: 16 gFiber: 7 g

125.   Chocolate Avocado Pudding

Preparation Time: 5 Minutes

Cooking Time: 0

Servings: 1

Ingredients:

1 avocado, halved

⅓ cup full-fat coconut milk

1 teaspoon vanilla extract

2 tablespoons unsweetened cocoa powder

5 or 6 drops liquid stevia

Directions:

Combine all the ingredients in a high-powered blender or food processor and blend until smooth. Serve immediately.

Nutrition:

Calories: 555 Cal

Fat: 47 g

Protein: 7 g

Carbs: 26 g

Fiber: 17 g

Conclusion

The Ketogenic diet is truly life changing. The diet improves your overall health and helps you lose the extra weight in a matter of days. The diet will show its multiple benefits even from the beginning and it will become your new lifestyle really soon.

As soon as you embrace the Ketogenic diet, you will start to live a completely new life. On the other hand, the vegetarian diet is such a healthy dietary option you can choose when trying to live healthy and also lose some weight.

The collection we bring to you today is actually a combination between the Ketogenic and vegetarian diets. You get to discover some amazing Ketogenic vegetarian dishes you can prepare in the comfort of your own home. All the dishes you found here follow both the Ketogenic and the vegetarian rules, they all taste delicious and rich and they are all easy to make.

You have already made the lifestyle decision to eat vegetarian foods, now add to that decision the choice to eat a keto lifestyle. By adding these two lifestyle choices together you will have the two most powerful weapons for weight loss and healthy living at your disposal. You now possess all the knowledge that you need in order to make this new lifestyle change to keto vegetarianism.

The different herbs and spices that were featured in this book have shown you how easy it is to create tasty dishes. You have recipes for many different sauces that will help to compliment your vegetarian choices without totally blowing your keto diet plan. You have recipes for delicious breakfasts, lunches, and dinners. We showed you how to create a sample meal plan that will teach you how easy it is to make good choices when it comes to the food that you put in your body. And we even gave you some recipes for desserts because we know you are human and life is so much better when it includes a little treat every now and then.

Most importantly we hope you now see that living the keto vegetarian lifestyle is not impossible. It might not be one of the easiest things you will ever do but it will enrich your life and your health far beyond anything you might ever have imagined.

We can assure you that such a combo is hard to find. So, start a keto diet with a vegetarian "touch" today. It will be both useful and fun!

So, what are you still waiting for? Get started with the Ketogenic diet and learn how to prepare the best and most flavored Ketogenic vegetarian dishes. Enjoy them all!

KETO VEGETARIAN COOKBOOK

A Simple Cookbook to Change Eating Habits with Low Carb Recipes for Beginners and Plant Based Meals for Boosting Your Energy and Improving Your Life

RIHANNA SMITH

TABLE OF CONTENCT

KETO VEGETARIAN COOKBOOK

Introduction

The keto diet is actually simple to understand. And at first, it seems difficult to put in practice, but it's actually a lot easier than most people think. We begin by considering what are called macronutrients. These are the general classes of calories in our diet. In other words, we can get calories from carbohydrates, fats, and proteins. So, when people are talking about "macros", they are just talking about the ratios of carbohydrates, fats, and proteins that are in your diet. The classification of the macro is-based on what molecules provided caloric energy. Before we get into the details of the keto diet, we need 0to understand the different macros and how they provide energy. Let's start with carbohydrates.

A carbohydrate is any molecule-based on sugar. Glucose is the simplest sugar of all. It's just one sugar molecule. Fructose is another simple sugar molecule that is found in fruit. There are more complex types of sugars, such as sucrose, which is a glucose and fructose molecule linked together. Beet and cane sugar are sucrose.

You can form long chains by linking up sugar molecules together. This is the basis of a starch. So, starch is really just a bunch of sugar molecules hooked up together. If you ever thought that eating potatoes was "healthy," and yet you gain weight eating them, this could be a clue as to why. When you get right down to it, while it does contain many valuable vitamins and minerals, a potato is really a bunch of sugar. However, when sugar molecules form chains, the body has to break them apart in order to get at the energy.

The body needs glucose for energy; when people talk about blood sugar, they are talking about glucose. So, eating a potato is a little better than eating pure sugar as far as blood sugar is concerned, because it takes a bit of time to break it apart during digestion. So, the rise of blood sugar is slower and more gradual. But the truth is for a lot of people the digestion of starchy foods causes a lot of health problems. We will talk about that later.

Some carbohydrates actually can't be digested by humans. These types of carbohydrates are known as dietary fiber. Dietary fiber can be helpful for the digestion of carbohydrates because the body has to break it apart in order to get at the carbohydrates that produce energy. For example, "whole grains" include indigestible components of the grain that help to slow the absorption of the carbohydrates in it that we can digest. For this reason, whole grains are often recommended for people with blood sugar problems, and for people on vegetarian diets, whole grains are often a major calorie source.

In the end, however, if you are prone to diabetes, whole grains can cause blood sugar problems. In some people, they can be almost as problematic as eating simple carbohydrates like white bread.

But no matter what type of carbohydrate-based food you eat—be it potatoes, berries, fruit, or bread—in the end, it's broken down into glucose that your body can use for energy.

Since many vegetarians and vegans get a lot of their protein from beans, we need to make a mental note about them. The truth is that beans contain carbohydrates. They also contain significant amounts of dietary fiber, and therefore they are better than just eating a slice of white bread (not to mention the high protein content).

However, on a keto diet, you're going to want to avoid consuming beans for the simple fact that we are going to strictly limit carbohydrates. Even though beans can be said to have complex carbohydrates due to the high dietary fiber content, in the end, they contain carbohydrates that are going to cause rising blood sugar.

A gram of carbohydrate provides 4 calories of energy.

The next macro in the diet are proteins. Protein is a source of energy, but in order for the body to use it, protein has to be broken down and repackaged into sugar. The liver can do this, and this takes time. Of course, your body also needs the amino acids to build muscle tissue and other structures that are important. So, protein by itself is hardly an ideal energy source, but each gram of protein does provide 4 calories of energy.

The last macro is fat. Fat is a very complex molecule, and as a result, it provides a large reservoir of energy. Intuitively, you probably have a sense that fat is an energy-packed food. It not only gives you more energy, but it also helps you to feel satiated. Feeling satiated is an important part of eating, when you don't feel satiated or don't feel satiated for very long, then you are going get in situations where you overeat in an effort to quell your hunger. Fat helps prevent this by leaving you feel more satisfied and for longer. A gram of fat provides 9 calories of energy, more than twice that we get from carbohydrates or proteins.

As we'll see later, the body can burn energy from fat rather than from sugar. The standard education has been that the body uses glucose for energy and that the body must have glucose. Now we are learning that this isn't true. In fact, the body may be designed to burn energy from fat. This is done by breaking fat down into component molecules that can be used for energy. They are called ketones.

What is Ketogenic Diet?

The globally known ketogenic diet is one of the most scientifically proven weight loss diets that is taking over the world. With its rising popularity due to the amazing benefits that a keto diet offers, such as rapid weight loss, prevents certain diseases, increased energy, and brain function. No wonder this diet is sweeping this nation!

- **Why so many people follow the ketogenic diet**

- **How to enter and sustain the state of ketosis**

- **How to know if you are in ketosis**

- **What do you eat and not eat on a standard ketogenic diet?**

Ready to start? Go ahead!

Why So Many People Are Following the Keto Diet?

The ketogenic diet currently is one of the most popular diets worldwide. It has gained popularity due to it being easy to follow than most diet trends and guarantees life-changing benefits. In a nutshell, the goal of the ketogenic diet is to deprive your body of carbohydrates in order to enter the metabolic state of ketosis.

The main fuel source of your body are carbohydrates, so starving your body of carbs forces the body to use alternative sources of fuel. When you eat foods high in carbs, it breaks down into glucose which is then absorbed and spread into the bloodstream to provide energy. When your intake of carbs is extremely low, which is somewhere between 20 grams to 50 grams per day, your metabolism begins to change. Instead of using glucose for energy, your body breaks down fats into ketones, which is then harvested as fuel for your brain and body.

In the ketogenic diet, you will reduce your carbohydrate intake and increase your fat and protein intake to produce ketones for fuel. The keto diet has attracted tons of people due to the host of benefits that comes once you reach ketosis. Some of the benefits including:

- Decreases hunger

- Faster weight loss

- Enhanced cognitive ability

- Better mental clarity

- Decrease inflammation

- Better sleep

- Reduces various diseases and conditions

How to Enter and Maintain the State of Ketosis

There are a number of ways to enter and maintain the state of ketosis. Here we will look how you can enter ketosis in order to reap the benefits:

1. Minimize Your Carb Intake

Depriving your body of carbs is the best way to go for reaching ketosis. The ketogenic diet in particular drastically reduces your carb intake and increases your fat intake which provides fuel. Over the long-term, the ketogenic diet has been proven to be the best way to go for maintaining ketosis.

2. Exercise More

Increasing your physical activity can help your body decrease glycogen. When glycogen is low, and not being replenished with foods high in carbs, the body looks to the alternative of burning fat for energy. So, increasing the intensity of your exercise can help you enter ketosis quicker.

3. Fasting

Fasting brings a number of benefits and is usually sued in combination with the keto diet to reach ketosis quicker. Going on a fast can help get rid of your carb intake and empty glycogen stores to enter ketosis faster. It can also assist you in maintaining the state of ketosis longer.

You can also try intermittent fasting which is a type of fasting that most keto dieters utilize. Several ways to try intermittent fasting are:

- Skipping meals – You can skip some of your meals during your day to extend your period of fasting (some people choose to skip breakfast and some choose to skip dinner)

- Eating windows – You can try to eat only within a specific time range. For example, some people eat only between 3pm to 6pm.

- Prolonged fast – You can also fast and eat something every other day. For example, you can go for an extended fasting period of 24 to 48 hours once a week.

4. Listen to your body

It is imperative to respect your appetite when attempting to reach ketosis. This implies that you should only eat when you're feeling hungry and don't binge on unhealthy foods. By eating only when we are hungry, we're reducing our food intake so that our body doesn't consume more food than it needs.

5. Drink plenty of water

A lot of people mistake thirst for hunger, and it's important to not make this error when you're following the keto diet. Try to drink water first before your meals and it will help you feel full. Try to drink water first before your meals and you may realize that you are actually full. Drinking loads of water can help clear your body of toxins and encourage the break down of fat to ketones.

How to Know if you Are in Ketosis?

There are a number of signs and symptoms that show you are in ketosis. If you are showing any of these symptoms below you have reached ketosis:

- If you are experiencing extreme thirst.

- If you have a dry mouth.

- If it looks like you have lost some weight.

- If you have smelly "keto" breath.

- If you can focus better

- If you are showing any signs or symptoms of the keto flu.

- If you are showing any signs of digestive problems.

Other ways you can check if you are in ketosis are using:

- Blood ketone meter: Using a blood ketone meter is one of the most accurate ways to evaluate the number of ketones within your body. It's best to evaluate your blood ketones while on an empty stomach usually in the early mornings. You can find blood ketone meters at your local pharmacy store or you can order online.

- Urine ketone strips: Urine ketone strips evaluate the ketones in your urine. You can find urine strips at your local pharmacy and follow the instructions according to the package to determine your ketone levels.

- Breathalyzer: Another way to determine whether or not you are in ketosis is using a ketone breathalyzer which checks out your breath. However, the only problem with using a breathalyzer is that drinking alcohol or coffee can affect the results of a breathalyzer.

What Do You Eat and Not Eat on a Standard Ketogenic Diet?

As we covered earlier, the goal of the ketogenic diet is to enter the state of ketosis. Ketosis can only be achieved once you deprive your body of carbohydrates. So you will avoid high carbohydrate foods and consume only foods that are low in carbs and high in healthy fats.

Also, you will need to decide on your macronutrient ratio for the keto diet. Your macronutrient ratio is the number of carbs, protein, and fats that you consume in relation to one another. On the standard ketogenic diet, it recommends the macronutrient ratio of:

- 75% fat

- 20% protein

- 5% carbohydrate

When you incorporate vegetarianism with the ketogenic diet, the macronutrients will change slightly.

FATS

On the ketogenic diet, it is imperative that you consume high amounts of healthy fats otherwise your body won't have fuel and you will not feel so great. There are some fats that are good for you while other fats are very unhealthy and should be avoided at all costs. Here are some of the absolute best fats to use when cooking on the keto diet:

- Coconut oil

- Olive oil

- Ghee

- Butter

- Lard

Unhealthy fats that you should avoid are the following:

- Margarine

- Vegetable oil

- Trans fats

PROTEIN

While fat is essential for the keto diet, you should not forget about protein. Protein is important for weight loss, maintain muscle mass and your overall health. Most people confuse the keto diet with a high-protein diet, but you will only consume a moderate amount of proteins. The amount of protein you consume daily will be determined by your body weight and your activity level. The more active you are, the more protein you will need.

While protein is important for the keto diet, you need to avoid eating too much protein. Eating too much protein will produce a hormone known as glucagon, which will convert protein into glucose. On the standard keto diet, the best sources of protein are from pasture-raised poultry, wild-caught fish, and other meat products. When you combine vegetarianism with the keto diet, obviously you cannot consume meat, so you will consume eggs, seeds, and nuts.

CARBOHYDRATES

The excess consumption of carbohydrates is dangerous because it raises your blood sugar level. If you are regularly eating plenty of carbs, your blood sugar will remain higher than normal levels which can lead to a number of problems. Most notably, it can lead to type 2 diabetes. On the standard keto diet, you will need to avoid the following:

- Flour

- Sugar

- Pasta

- Bread

- Beans

- Legumes

On the keto diet, 5% of your calories will be coming from carbohydrates. The best sources of carbohydrates come from low-carb vegetables such as spinach, broccoli, zucchini, asparagus, etc.

Advantage of Keto Diet

The advantages of keto diet are almost similar to other diets based on low carb intake; the only difference is that the keto diet is more powerful and efficient in its benefits. In simpler words, the keto diet is a low carb diet plan with super-charged powers compared to its competitors and has maximum benefits to offer for the users. A few of its major benefits are as follows:

Weight Loss:

The fact that the body uses fats as an energy source logically explain how the keto diet is beneficial in weight loss. Fat loss is stimulated as the insulin levels are dropped low. This situation provides an ideal situation for drastic fat loss, resulting in weight loss effectively without hunger. It is to note that, above 20 modern types of research has verified that the keto diet is more effective than other similar diet plans in its weight loss factor.

Controlled Appetite:

This control of appetite also results in more effective weight loss. It also eases the intermittent fasting, stimulates the reversal of type-2 diabetes apart from stimulating weight loss. It is also very feasible financially as it reduces your expenditure on food due to less hunger.

The lower urge to eat food or controlled appetite also helps a lot to avoid sugar and food addiction alongside eating disorders like bulimia etc. The feeling of satisfaction is an integral part of the solution. Food becomes a friend and a fueling source instead of an enemy with the ketogenic diet plan.

Surplus Energy and Mental Boosting:

The process of ketosis provides a steady flow of energy in the form of ketones to the brain resulting in avoiding blood sugar swings. This results in improvement in mental focus and concentration and also clear away brain fog too. The main reason for the popularity of the keto diet is tits benefits regarding mental health and focus. These benefits can be easily experienced while being in ketosis. During ketosis, the human brain is provided with surplus energy round the clock in the form of ketones instead of carbs which is the reason for the improved mental performance of the human body.

Reversing Type-2 Diabetes & Controlling Blood Sugar:

Although ketogenic diet is not scientifically acknowledged as a long-term solution to type 2 diabetes, it is credited to the fact that keto diet lowers down blood sugar levels in the body and also lowers the negative role of higher insulin levels. The fact that keto diet is very efficient in reversing type-2 diabetes also suggests that it is very helpful in avoiding it in the first place apart from reversing pre-diabetic conditions.

Improvement in Health Markers:

Lower carb intake results in improvement in critical health markers like blood sugar levels, cholesterol levels (triglycerides and HDL) and in blood pressure. These health markers are associated with metabolic syndrome, weight improvements, reversal of type-2 diabetes and waist circumference etc.

Stomach Improvement:

Keto diet has many efficiency improvements in stomach health. It lowers cramps and pains alongside less or entirely no gas at all in the stomach. It can be experienced within the initial 2-3 days of following the ketogenic diet plan. FODMAP contains a high amount of carbs and they start fermentation in the small intestine which leads to bloating and gas. The gut walls are unable to absorb them properly and cause the fluid stuck in the intestine thus resulting in diarrhea. The keto diet is a much low FODMAP diet and acts as an anti-IBS approach. The slow removal of carbs from your diet improves your digestive system befittingly.

Improvement in Physical Strength:

Ketogenic diet improves physical strength and endurance a lot due to the provision of a regular and constant supply of energy from fats. Energy due to carbs (glycogen) in the body only for a few hours of high-level exercising, contrary to this the energy from fat sources lasts for weeks or even months in the body and enhances the physical performances of the body.

Epilepsy Treatment:

The keto diet is very beneficial for the treatment of epilepsy since the 1920s. In the initial days it was used for children only but now it has also been applied to adults and has shown improvements in them. With ketogenic diet, patients of epilepsy either take less or even not a single medication for their treatment without the fear of any seizures. This also lowers the side effects of drugs by lowering drug intake and plays a role in mental health improvement.

The most beneficial thing about the keto diet is that it lets epilepsy patients stop taking much lower medications for the disease and yet able to control epilepsy. In some cases, they can even get rid of this medication without having the risk of any seizures. Anti-epilepsy drugs have side effects like concentration loss, drowsiness etc. which can be evaded with the keto diet by getting rid of the medications.

Additional Benefits:

Apart from the above-mentioned advantages, there are certain benefits which are life-changing for certain people. The lower intake of carbs has many advantages like migraine control, lesser acne issues, blood pressure controlling and even aids in certain mental health complications. A few additional benefits of the ketogenic diet are listed as below:

- Lesser Acne

- Reversing PCOS (Polycystic Ovary Syndrome)

- Fever Heartburn

- Fewer Migraine Attacks

- Treatment of Brain Cancer

- Lesser Sugar Cravings

- Curing Alzheimer

- BP level controlling

Appetizers and Starters Recipes

126.   Keto Vegan Lasagna Rolls

Preparation Time: 20 Minutes

Cook Time: 20 Minutes

Servings: 10

Ingredients

Rolls;

Pepper and salt to taste

1 teaspoon of coconut oil

1 zucchini

1 eggplant

Half a cup of organic tomato sauce

Cashew cheese;

Water

A pinch of salt

A cup of raw cashews nuts

Extras;

Half a teaspoon of salt

Half a teaspoon of garlic powder

Directions:

For the cashew cheese;

Add a pinch of sea salt into a bowl of water, put the cashews in and allow them to soak for 8 hours or if you have the time, soak them overnight or for a full day.

Drain the water from the cashew and place them in a food processor, add garlic powder and process until smooth, then season with a pinch or two of salt.

Blend again until the cashews become very creamy, if at this point they are too thick or pasty, you can thin it out with some water.

Pour the creamy blend into a jar and refrigerate.

For lasagna;

Cut the zucchini and eggplant lengthwise into thin strips.

Sprinkle some salt on one side of the slices and set them aside to rest for about 10 minutes. This is to draw out excess moisture from the zucchini and eggplant strips.

Use a paper towel to pay the vegetable strips dry, so as to get rid of excess moisture.

Pour oil into a medium sized pan, set over medium heat and allow to simmer for a minute, then add the strips.

Fry on each side for 2 minutes, until they are lightly browned. Repeat this process for all the strips then set aside.

Once they are ready, place the strips on a plate, and scoop some cashew cheese in the middle of each strip.

Top with a nice drizzle of organic tomato sauce over each strip, sprinkle some salt and pepper and roll the strips.

Serve and enjoy.

Nutrition:

Calories: 97 Cal

Fat: 4 g

Fiber: 2 g

Carbs: 6 g

Protein: 2 g

127. Stuffed Avocados

Preparation Time: 15 Minutes

Cooking Time: 0

Servings: 6

Ingredients:

Vegan Mayo

3 avocados (halved and seed removed)

1 jalapeño (seed removed and finely diced)

1 tablespoon of lemon juice

Salt and pepper to taste

3 grape tomatoes (diced)

A quarter teaspoon of garlic powder

A quarter piece of cucumber (diced)

1 small red onion (diced)

A quarter piece of orange bell pepper (cored and diced)

Directions: Use the lemon juice to marinate the flash if the avocados to stop them from browning. Put the cucumber, bell peppers, onions, tomatoes, garlic, jalapeño, and enough mayo into a bowl, stir until well combined. Fill the avocados with the vegetable mixture, add a small amount of lemon juice and a sprinkle of salt, then serve.

Nutrition: Calories: 167 Cal - Fat: 6 g

Fiber: 7 g - Carbs: 5 g - Protein: 3 g

128. Keto Vegan Cashew Cheese

Preparation Time: 5 Minutes

Cooking Time: 10 Minutes

Servings: 7

Ingredients

A quarter teaspoon of dried thyme

1 clove of garlic (grated)

Half a teaspoon of dried parsley

1 teaspoon of kosher salt

2 tablespoons of coconut oil

A quarter teaspoon of dried dill

A quarter teaspoon of dried pepper

2 tablespoons of lemon juice

1 teaspoon of dried basil leaves

Almond crackers (for serving)

1 teaspoon of dried chives

1 cup of raw cashews

Directions:

Soak the cashews in water overnight or for 8 hours, then drain.

Put the lemon juice, soaked cashews, coconut oil, garlic, pepper and salt into a food processor, blend for 7-10 minutes using the S-blade attachment until a thick paste is formed.

Pour cashew cheese into a medium sized bowl, add the dried herbs and stir until well combined.

Line any small bowl with Saran wrap and pour the cashew cheese in it, fold the edges of the saran wrap and refrigerate for two hours.

Serve with almond crackers.

Nutrition:

Calories: 197 Cal

Fat: 7 g

Fiber: 7.6 g

Carbs: 5.6 g

Protein: 4.2 g

129. Baba Ghanoush

Preparation Time: 10 Minutes

Cooking Time: 25 Minutes

Servings: 2

Ingredients:

Half a teaspoon of fine sea salt

A quarter cup of full fat coconut milk

1 large eggplant

2 tablespoons of Thai green curry paste

2 limes

A quarter cup of fresh cilantro (chopped)

Directions:

Set your broiler to high and place the racks at least 6 inches from the heat source.

Cut the eggplant in half, place on a baking sheet with the cut side facing down, then poke holes in the eggplant using a fork.

Broil the eggplant until soft, that is for about 25 minutes, then set aside to cool.

Grate two teaspoons of lime zest , then squeeze one tablespoon of juice from the lines.

Remove the flesh from the eggplants using a spoon, then put them in a food processor and blend until smooth.

Add the coconut milk, curry paste, lime juice and zest, cilantro and salt to taste, blend again until smooth.

Serve warm or cold with some crackers or vegetables.

Nutrition:

Calories: 57 Cal

Fat: 6 g

Fiber: 4 g

Carbs: 8 g

Protein: 4 g

130. Avocado Fries

Preparation Time: 10 Minutes

Cooking Time: 15 Minutes

Servings: 4

Ingredients: A quarter cup of almond milk

Half a cup of almond flour

1 large avocado (not too ripe)

1 teaspoon of Cajun seasoning

Directions:

Preheat your oven to 450F.

Cut the avocado in half, pit and cut into wedges. Put the Cajun Seasoning and almond flour, stir to combine. Pour the almond milk into a bowl and set aside.

Put the avocado slices into the milk, then put it in the flour mixture, making sure to coat the avocado completely. Line a baking sheet with parchment paper.

Place the coated avocados in the baking sheet, place in the oven and cook for 15 minutes.

Once the avocados are golden, remove them from the oven and set aside to cool for a few minutes before serving, but they are better when served hot.

Enjoy with some vegan mayo.

Nutrition: Calories: 207 Cal Fat: 6 g

Fiber: 5 g Carbs: 7.9 g Protein: 4 g

131. Keto Vegan "Cheese" Sticks

Preparation Time: 5 Minutes

Cooking Time: 7 Minutes

Servings: 7

Ingredients: 1 tablespoon of olive oil

2 tablespoons of nutritional yeast

2 cans of hearts of palm

A quarter teaspoon of garlic (minced)

2 tablespoons of soy flour

3 tablespoons of water

1 teaspoon of taco seasoning

A quarter teaspoon of black pepper

A pinch of salt

Directions: Preheat your oven to 375F.

Line a baking sheet with parchment paper. Drain and rinse the hearts of palm, put in a bowl then set aside. In a big bowl, mix the water , olive oil and dry ingredients together until fully combined and smooth. Coat the hearts of palm in the mixture then place them on the pre lined baking sheet. Put in the oven and bake for 25 minutes or until the coating is completely firm to the touch. Serve with marinara sauce and enjoy!

Nutrition: Calories: 57 Cal Fat: 3 g

Fiber: 4 g Carbs: 3 g Protein: 3 g

132. Keto Vegan Crack Bars

Preparation Time: 2 Minutes

Cooking Time: 10 Minutes

Servings: 20

Ingredients

1 cup of melted coconut oil

2 cups of shredded coconut flakes (unsweetened)

A quarter cup of liquid stevia

Half a cup of cranberries (unsweetened)

Directions:

Put the cranberries and coconut into a food processor, pulse on high until fully combined and an uneven paste is formed.

Put the cranberry mixture, stevia and coconut oil into a large mixing bowl, mix until fully combined.

Pour batter into a pre lined 8 by 8-inch baking tray.

Wet your hands and press the batter firmly into the tray.

Refrigerate for 8- 24 hours.

Cut into small squares and serve.

Nutrition: Calories: 97 Cal

Fat: 3 g Fiber: 7 g

Carbs: 4 g

Protein: 3 g

133.   Vegetable Dip

Preparation Time: 10 Minutes

Cooking Time: 5 Minutes

Servings: 12

Ingredients:

2 tablespoons of dill leaves

A quarter cup of walnut cheese

1 teaspoon of lemon juice

1 cup of sour cream

2 tablespoons of chives (roughly chopped)

1 clove of garlic

A quarter cup of parsley leaves

Directions:

Put all the ingredients into a food processor, blend until smooth

Pour into a bowl and serve with your favorite vegetables and enjoy.

Nutrition:

Calories: 56 Cal

Fat: 4 g

Fiber: 1 g

Carbs: 4 g

Protein: 3 g

134.   Mongolian Stir Fry

Preparation Time: 5 Minutes

Cooking Time: 4 Minutes

Servings: 4

Ingredients: 1 tablespoon minced ginger

1 teaspoon minced garlic

1 tablespoon avocado oil

4 tablespoons soy sauce

1 teaspoon chili flakes

1 teaspoon cornstarch

1 tablespoon brown sugar 8 tablespoon water

½ teaspoon cayenne pepper

1-pound seitan, chopped

Directions:

In the mixing bowl whisk together minced ginger, minced garlic, avocado oil, soy sauce, chili flakes, cornstarch, brown sugar, cayenne pepper, and water. Preheat instant pot bowl on Sauté mode until hot. Transfer ginger mixture in the instant pot and cook it for 1 minute. Then add chopped seitan and stir well. Close the lid and set Manual mode (high pressure) for 1 minute. Use quick pressure release. Mix up the side dish well before serving.

Nutrition: Calories: 59 Cal Carbs: 5.6 g

Fat: 0.9 g Protein: 6.6 g

135. Mushroom "Bacon"

Preparation Time: 5 Minutes

Cooking Time: 2 Minutes

Servings: 5

Ingredients:

6 oz shiitake mushrooms

1 teaspoon salt

¼ teaspoon cayenne pepper

1 tablespoon olive oil

Directions:

Slice the mushrooms onto bacon shape strips and sprinkle every strip with olive oil, cayenne pepper, and salt.

Then place mushroom "bacon" in the instant pot and close the lid.

Set Manual mode (high pressure) and cook mushrooms for 2 minutes. Then use quick pressure release. The time of cooking depends on mushroom strips size.

Nutrition:

Calories: 43 Cal

Carbs: 4.7 g

Fat: 2.9 g

Protein: 0.5 g

136. Crushed Baby Potatoes

Preparation Time: 10 Minutes

Cooking Time: 10 Minutes

Servings: 2

Ingredients:

1 ½ cup baby potatoes

1 teaspoon salt

4 tablespoons olive oil

1 tablespoon dried rosemary

1 teaspoon dried oregano

Directions:

Wash baby potatoes carefully and crush with the help of the knife.

Then sprinkle the crushed potatoes with salt, olive oil, dried rosemary, and oregano.

Shake well until homogenous.

Transfer potatoes in the instant pot and close the lid.

Cook the meal on Manual mode (high pressure) for 4 minutes.

Then use natural pressure release for 5 minutes. Don't mix up potatoes anymore.

Nutrition:

Calories: 325 Cal Carbs: 19.2 g

Fat: 28.4 g Protein: 2.1 g

137. Bang Bang Broccoli

Preparation Time: 10 Minutes

Cooking Time: 4 Minutes

Servings: 2

Ingredients:

2 tablespoons vegan mayo

1 teaspoon chili paste

1 tablespoon Maple syrup

1 cup broccoli

¼ cup almond milk

1 teaspoon cornstarch

2 tablespoons wheat flour

1 teaspoon olive oil

1/3 cup panko bread crumbs

1 tablespoon lemon juice

½ cup water for cooking

Directions:

For the sauce: whisk together vegan mayo and chili paste.

For the broccoli batter: in the separated bowl whisk together almond milk, wheat flour, olive oil, cornstarch, and lemon juice.

Cut broccoli into the florets and dip into the batter.

Then coat every broccoli floret in the panko bread crumbs.

Pour water in the instant pot bowl and insert rack.

Place coated broccoli on the rack and close the lid.

Cook the vegetables on Manual mode (High pressure) for 4 minutes. Use quick pressure release.

Transfer the cooked broccoli in the bowl and sprinkle with sauce.

Nutrition:

Calories: 280 Cal

Carbs: 33.7 g

Fat: 14.7 g

Protein 5.4 g

138. Tikka Masala with Cauliflower

Preparation Time: 10 Minutes

Cooking Time: 10 Minutes

Servings: 4

Ingredients:

1 teaspoon garam masala

½ teaspoon salt

1 cup cauliflower, chopped

1/3 cup coconut yogurt

1 teaspoon ground cumin

½ teaspoon ground coriander

1 onion, diced

½ teaspoon garlic, diced

¼ teaspoon minced ginger

1 cup tomatoes, canned

Directions:

Set instant pot on Sauté mode.

Add olive oil, diced onion, garlic, and minced ginger.

Then sprinkle the mixture with ground cumin, coriander, salt, and garam masala.

Mix up well.

Add canned tomatoes and mix up well. Sauté the mixture for 5 minutes.

After this, add chopped cauliflower and stir well.

Close the lid and seal it. Cook the meal on Manual mode (High pressure) for 3 minutes.

Then use quick pressure release and open the lid.

Add coconut yogurt and mix up well. Serve the meal hot

Nutrition:

Calories: 67 Carbs: 7.2 g

Fat: 4.1 g Protein: 1.7 g

Vegetable En Papillote

Preparation Time: 10 Minutes

Cooking Time: 3 Minutes

Servings: 4

Ingredients: 1 cup baby carrot

½ cup green beans

1 teaspoon dried rosemary 1 teaspoon salt

1 tablespoon avocado oil

1 garlic clove, diced

1 teaspoon fresh oregano

1 tablespoon lemon juice

1 teaspoon turmeric

Directions:

In the mixing bowl mix up together baby carrot and green beans.

Sprinkle the vegetables with dried rosemary, salt, avocado oil, garlic, oregano, lemon juice, and turmeric. Shake the ingredients well.

Then Wrap the vegetables in the baking paper and transfer in the instant pot. Close the lid and seal it. Cook the vegetables on Manual mode (High pressure) for 3 minutes.

Then allow natural pressure release for 5 minutes and remove vegetables from the baking paper.

Nutrition:

Calories: 30 Cal Carbs: 5.8 g Fat: 0.7 g

Protein: 0.7 g

139. Fragrant Bulgur

Preparation Time: 5 Minutes

Cooking Time: 19 Minutes

Servings: 3

Ingredients:

1 cup bulgur

1 teaspoon tomato paste

2 cups of water

1 teaspoon olive oil

1 teaspoon salt

Directions:

Preheat instant pot on Sauté mode and add olive oil.

Place bulgur in the oil and stir well. Sauté it for 4 minutes.

Then add tomato paste and salt. Stir well.

Add water and mix up bulgur until you get a homogenous liquid mixture.

Close the lid and set Manual mode (low pressure).

Cook bulgur for 15 minutes.

The bulgur will be cooked when it soaks all the liquid.

Nutrition:

Calories: 174 Cal Carbs: 35.8 g

Fat: 2.2 gProtein: 5.8 g

140. Baked Apples

Preparation Time: 5 Minutes

Cooking Time: 9 Minutes

Servings: 6

Ingredients: 4 red apples, chopped

1 teaspoon ground cinnamon

1 tablespoon brown sugar

1 teaspoon maple syrup ¼ cup cashew milk

Directions:

Place apples in the instant pot and sprinkle with ground cinnamon, brown sugar, and maple syrup. Close the lid and set Sauté mode. Cook the apples for 5 minutes. Then add cashew milk and mix up the side dish well.

Cook it for 4 minutes more.

Nutrition:

Calories: 88 Cal Carbs: 23.1 g Fat: 0.4 g

Protein: 0.4 g

141. Scalloped Potatoes

Preparation Time: 15 Minutes

Cooking Time: 4 Minutes

Servings: 4

Ingredients: 4 potatoes, peeled, sliced

1 cup almond milk

1 teaspoon nutritional yeast

1 teaspoon dried rosemary

½ teaspoon salt

1 teaspoon garlic powder

1 teaspoon cashew butter

1 teaspoon ground nutmeg

Directions:

Mix up together nutritional yeast, dried rosemary, salt, garlic powder, and ground nutmeg. Whisk together almond milk and spice mixture. Grease the instant pot bowl with cashew butter. Place the sliced potatoes inside instant pot bowl by layers. Then pour almond milk mixture over the potatoes and close the lid. Cook scalloped potatoes on Manual mode (High pressure) for 4 minutes. Then allow natural pressure release for 10 minutes. Sprinkle the cooked meal with your favorite vegan cheese if desired.

Nutrition:

Calories: 302 Carbs: 38.5 g Fat: 15.5 g

Protein: 5.7 g

142. Glazed White Onions

Preparation Time: 5 Minutes

Cooking Time: 20 Minutes

Servings: 4

Ingredients:

3 white onions, peeled, sliced

1 tablespoon sugar

½ teaspoon ground black pepper

3 tablespoons coconut oil

½ teaspoon baking soda

Directions:

Set Sauté mode and preheat instant pot until hot.

Toss coconut oil and melt it.

When the coconut oil is liquid, add sugar, baking soda, and ground black pepper. Stir the mixture gently.

Add sliced onions and mix the ingredients up.

Close the lid and sauté onions for 15 minutes.

When the side dish is cooked it will have a light brown color and tender texture.

Nutrition:

Calories: 133 Cal

Carbs: 10.9 g Fat: 10.3 g

Protein: 0.9 g

143. Spicy Garlic

Preparation Time: 10 Minutes

Cooking Time: 10 Minutes

Servings: 4

Ingredients:

4 garlic bulbs, trimmed

2 teaspoons olive oil

½ teaspoon salt

¼ teaspoon chili flakes

½ cup water, for cooking

Directions:

Pour water in the instant pot and insert rack.

Place garlic bulbs on the rack and sprinkle with olive oil, salt, and chili flakes.

Close the lid and set Poultry mode.

Cook garlic for 10 minutes. Then allow natural pressure release for 5 minutes more.

Serve the garlic when it reaches room temperature.

Nutrition:

Calories: 35 Cal

Carbs: 3 g

Fat: 2.3 g

Protein: 0 g

144. Flavored Tomato and Okra Mix

Preparation Time: 10 Minutes

Cooking Time: 30 Minutes

Servings: 6

Ingredients:

1 cup scallions, chopped

1-pound cherry tomatoes, halved

2 cups okra, sliced

2 tablespoons avocado oil

4 garlic cloves, chopped

2 teaspoons oregano, dried

A pinch of salt and black pepper

2 teaspoons cumin, ground

1 cup veggie stock

2 tablespoons tomato passata

Directions:

Heat up a pan with the oil over medium heat, add the scallions and the garlic and sauté for 5 minutes.

Add the tomatoes, the okra and the other ingredients, toss, cook over medium heat for 25 minutes, divide between plates and serve as a side dish.

Nutrition: Calories: 84 Cal Fat: 2.1 g Fiber: 5.4 g Carbs: 14.8 g Protein: 4 g

145. Orange Scallions and Brussels Sprouts

Preparation Time: 10 Minutes

Cooking Time: 25 Minutes

Servings: 4

Ingredients:

1-pound Brussels sprouts, trimmed and halved

1 cup scallions, chopped

Zest of 1 lime, grated

1 tablespoon olive oil

¼ cup orange juice

2 tablespoons stevia

A pinch of salt and black pepper

Directions:

Heat up a pan with the oil over medium heat, add the scallions and sauté for 5 minutes.

Add the sprouts and the other ingredients, toss, cook over medium heat for 20 minutes more, divide the mix between plates and serve.

Nutrition:

Calories: 193 Cal

Fat: 4 g

Fiber: 1 g

Carbs: 8 gProtein: 10 g

Breakfast Recipes

146. Cauliflower Waffles

Preparation Time: 10 Minutes

Cooking Time: 10 Minutes

Servings: 4

Ingredients:

½ large head cauliflower, riced

1 cup mozzarella cheese, finely shredded

1 cup packed collard greens

1 egg

1/4 cup Parmesan cheese

1 tablespoon sesame seed

2 stalks green onion

2 tablespoons olive oil

2 teaspoons fresh thyme, chopped

1 teaspoon garlic powder

½ teaspoon ground black pepper

½ teaspoon salt

Directions:

Grind cauliflower florets with spring onion, collard greens, and thyme in a food processor.

Toss this mixture with 1 cup Mozzarella cheese, egg, /4 cup Parmesan Cheese. 1 tablespoon olive oil, 1 tablespoon sesame seeds, ½ teaspoon black pepper, ½ teaspoon salt, and 1 teaspoon garlic powder in a mixing bowl.

Once the mixture forms an even mixture add a ¼ cup of this batter in the waffle iron.

Let the batter cook in the iron as per the machine's instructions.

Use the remaining batter to make more waffles.

Enjoy fresh.

Nutrition:

Calories: 203 Cal

Fat: 15.3 g

Carbs: 5 g

Protein: 14.6 g

147. Morning Bullet Coffee

Preparation Time: 10 Minutes

Cooking Time: 5 Minutes

Servings: 2

Ingredients: 1 oz. cacao butter

2 tablespoons coconut oil

2 tablespoons almond butter

1/4 cup almond milk

2 cups of coffee, brewed

Directions:

Add cocoa butter, almond butter and coconut oil to a jug and heat them in the microwave for 20 seconds. Add almond milk and heat more for 30 seconds. Stir in coffee and blend well using a handheld blender until foamy.

Serve fresh.

Nutrition:

Calories: 171 Cal Fat: 10.3 g Carbs: 7 g

Protein: 14.3 g

148. Tofu Quiche Cups

Preparation Time: 10 Minutes

Cooking Time: 35 Minutes

Servings: 4

Ingredients: 1 (14 oz) block extra firm tofu

3 tablespoon water

2 teaspoon garlic seasoning

1 tablespoon sugar- free ketchup

2 tablespoon dijon mustard

1 tablespoon lemon juice

1 tablespoon arrowroot powder

1/2 cup nutritional yeast

3.5 cups leafy greens

Directions:

Let your oven to preheat at 350 degrees F. Layer a muffin tin with muffin liners. Blend everything except leafy greens, in a blender until smooth. If the mixture is too thick, add few drops of water and blend again.

Stir in leafy greens and mix until it forms an even mixture. Divide the prepared batter in the muffin tin and bake for 35 minutes until golden brown.

Enjoy warm and fresh.

Nutrition:

Calories: 231 Cal Fat: 14.3 g

Carbs: 3.7 g Protein: 7.6 g

149.   Cinnamon & Pecan Porridge

Preparation Time: 10 Minutes

Cooking Time: 5 Minutes

Servings: 2

Ingredients: 1/4 cup coconut milk

3/4 cup unsweetened almond milk

1/4 cup almond butter, roasted

1 tablespoon coconut oil

2 tablespoon whole chia seeds

2 tablespoon hemp seeds

1/4 cup pecans, chopped

1/4 cup unsweetened coconut, toasted

1/2 teaspoon cinnamon

Stevia to taste

Directions:

Mix coconut milk with almond butter, almond butter and coconut oil in a saucepan. Cook the mixture on a simmer over medium heat then add chia seeds, pecans, cinnamon, stevia, hemp seeds, and toasted coconut. Mix well and set it aside for 10 minutes approximately then divide it in the serving bowls. Garnish with coconut shred.

Serve fresh.

Nutrition:

Calories: 108 Cal Fat: 9 g

Carbs: 2.7 g Protein: 6 g

150.   Superfood Breakfast Bowl

Preparation Time: 10 Minutes

Cooking Time: 0

Servings: 1

Ingredients:

1 cup almond milk

2 tablespoon chia seeds

1/4 cup protein powder

5 tablespoon hemp seeds

2 tablespoon unsweetened coconut flakes

¼ cup mixed berries

1 tablespoon pecans, chopped

1 tablespoon walnuts, chopped

Directions:

Add protein powder, milk, hemp seeds, chia seeds and coconut to a mason jar.

Seal the jar and mix well then place the jar in the fridge for overnight.

Garnish with chopped nuts and berries.

Serve fresh.

Nutrition:

Calories: 231 Cal

Fat: 19.3 g

Carbs: 2.7 g

Protein: 32.6 g

151.   Strawberry Chia Pudding

Preparation Time: 10 Minutes

Cooking Time: 0

Servings: 2

Ingredients: 1 ½ cup of coconut milk

2 cups strawberries, fresh

½ tablespoon almond butter

2 pinches sea salt   Stevia, to taste

½ cup chia seeds

1 tablespoon MCT coconut oil

Garnish: 1 handful of berries

4 tablespoons keto granola

Directions:

Blend strawberries, coconut milk, salt and almond butter in a food processor.

Add stevia to sweeten the mixture.

Spread the chia seeds in the bowl and pour the strawberry mixture over chia seeds.

Refrigerate this bowl overnight until it thickens.

Garnish with your favorite berries.

Enjoy fresh.

Nutrition:

Calories: 118 Cal Fat: 9.3 g

Carbs: 1.7 g Protein: 12.6 g

152.   Blueberry Coconut Porridge

Preparation Time: 10 Minutes

Cooking Time: 0

Servings: 2

Ingredients: Porridge

1/4 cup ground flaxseed

1 cup almond milk 1 teaspoon cinnamon

1 teaspoon vanilla extract

1/4 cup coconut flour

liquid stevia, to taste

1 pinch salt

Toppings

¼ cup blueberries 2 tablespoon butter

2 tablespoon pumpkin seeds

1 oz. shaved coconut

Directions:

Warm almond milk in a saucepan then adds flaxseed, salt, cinnamon, and coconut flour. Mix well until smooth. Cook until it bubbles. Add vanilla extract and liquid stevia.Mix well then garnish with desired toppings blueberries, cold butter, shaved coconut, and pumpkin seeds. Serve fresh.

Nutrition:

Calories: 231 Cal Fat: 13.3 g

Carbs: 4 g Protein: 14.6 g

153. Raspberry Pancakes

Preparation Time: 10 Minutes

Cooking Time: 8 Minutes

Servings: 4

Ingredients: 1 teaspoon coconut flour

1/4 teaspoon baking powder

1/16 teaspoon Stevia

1/4 teaspoon cinnamon

1 tablespoon coconut oil 1 pinch salt

1/4 cup almond flour

1 tablespoon raspberries

2 tablespoons almond milk

Directions:

Blend all the dry items in a food processor then add the wet ingredients.

Fold in raspberries and mix well until smooth.

Warm-up a tablespoon of coconut oil in a flat pan and add a dollop of raspberry batter.

Spread it into a pancake and cook for 2 minutes per side.

Use the remaining batter to make more pancakes.

Enjoy fresh.

Nutrition:

Calories: 91 Fat: 13.3g Carbs: 7.3g

Protein: 22.6g

154. Raspberry Chia Pudding

Preparation Time: 10 Minutes

Cooking Time: 0

Servings: 1

Ingredients:

1 cup fresh raspberries

1 cup of coconut milk

1/2 cup almond milk

1/2 cup whole chia seeds

3 teaspoon unsweetened vanilla extract

Stevia to taste

Directions:

Blend raspberries with water and coconut milk in a food processor.

Keep few raspberries aside for garnishing.

Add chia seeds, vanilla and low carb sweetener to the raspberry mixture.

Mix well and refrigerate the pudding overnight.

Garnish with raspberries and serve fresh.

Nutrition:

Calories: 153 Cal Fat: 5.3 g

Carbs: 4.4 g

Protein: 4.6 g

155.   Chia Berry Yogurt Parfaits

Preparation Time: 10 Minutes

Cooking Time: 0

Servings: 2

Ingredients:

Chia pudding:

1/2 cup heavy cream

1/3 cup chia seeds

1/4 teaspoon vanilla powder

1/4 teaspoon ground cinnamon

2/3 cup water

1 tablespoon powdered Erythritol

LAYERS:

1 cup full-fat yogurt

1 cup mixed frozen berries

Coconut & seed crumble:

2 tablespoon pumpkin seeds

1/3 cup flaked coconut, toasted

2 tablespoon sunflower seeds

Directions:

Add all the ingredients for chia pudding to a jar and leave it in the refrigerator overnight.

Defrost the berries and crush them in a bowl to make a paste.

Prepare the crumble by mixing all the ingredients in a separate bowl.

Assemble the parfaits by adding layers of crushed berries and yogurt in the serving glass.

Serve fresh.

Nutrition:

Calories: 211 Cal

Fat: 14.3 g

Carbs: 5 g

Protein: 11.6g

156.   Warm Quinoa Breakfast Bowl

Preparation Time: 5 Minutes

Cooking Time: 0

Servings: 4

Ingredients

3 cups freshly cooked quinoa

1⅓ cups unsweetened soy or almond milk

2 bananas, sliced

1 cup raspberries

1 cup blueberries

½ cup chopped raw walnuts

¼ cup maple syrup

Directions

Preparing the Ingredients

Divide the ingredients among 4 bowls, starting with a base of ¾ cup quinoa, ⅓ cup milk, ½ banana, ¼ cup raspberries, ¼ cup blueberries, and 2 tablespoons walnuts.

Drizzle 1 tablespoon of maple syrup over the top of each bowl.

Nutrition:

Calories: 201 Cal

Fat: 15.3 g

Carbs: 3 g

Protein: 8.6 g

157. Banana Bread Rice Pudding

Preparation Time: 5 Minutes

Cooking Time: 50 Minutes

Servings: 4

Ingredients

1 cup brown rice

1½ cups water

1½ cups nondairy milk

3 tablespoons sugar (omit if using a sweetened nondairy milk)

2 teaspoons pumpkin pie spice or ground cinnamon

2 bananas

3 tablespoons chopped walnuts or sunflower seeds (optional)

Directions

Preparing the Ingredients.

In a medium pot, combine the rice, water, milk, sugar, and pumpkin pie spice. Bring to a boil over high heat, turn the heat to low, and cover the pot. Simmer, stirring occasionally, until the rice is soft and the liquid is absorbed. White rice takes about 20 minutes; brown rice takes about 50 minutes.

Smash the bananas and stir them into the cooked rice. Serve topped with walnuts (if using). Leftovers will keep refrigerated in an airtight container for up to 5 days.

Nutrition:

Calories: 479 Cal

Protein: 9 g

Fat: 13 g

Carbs: 86 g

Fiber: 7 g

158. Apple and Cinnamon Oatmeal

Preparation Time: 10 Minutes

Cook Time:10 Minutes

Servings: 2

Ingredients

1¼ cups apple cider

1 apple, peeled, cored, and chopped

⅔ cup rolled oats

1 teaspoon ground cinnamon

1 tablespoon pure maple syrup or agave (optional)

Directions

Preparing the Ingredients.

In a medium saucepan, bring the apple cider to a boil over medium-high heat. Stir in the apple, oats, and cinnamon.

Bring the cereal to a boil and turn down heat to low. Simmer until the oatmeal thickens, 3 to 4 minutes. Spoon into two bowls and sweeten with maple syrup, if using. Serve hot.

Nutrition:

Calories: 216 Cal

Fat: 8.3 g

Carbs:7 g

Protein: 9.6g

159. Cinnamon Muffins

Preparation Time: 15 Minutes

Cooking Time: 10 Minutes

Servings: 20

Ingredients:

½ cup coconut oil, melted

½ cup pumpkin puree

½ cup almond butter

1 tbsp cinnamon

1 tsp baking powder

2 scoops vanilla protein powder

½ cup almond flour

Directions:

Preheat the oven to 180 C/ 350 F.

Spray muffin tray with cooking spray and set aside.

Add all dry ingredients into the large bowl and mix well.

Add wet ingredients and mix until well combined. Pour batter into the prepared muffin tray and bake in preheated oven for 15 minutes.

Serve and enjoy.

Nutrition:

Calories: 80 Cal Fat: 7.1 g Carbs: 1.6 g

Protein: 3.5 g

160. Chocolate Strawberry Milkshake

Preparation Time: 5 Minutes

Cooking Time: 0

Servings: 2

Ingredients:

1 cup ice cubes

¼ cup unsweetened cocoa powder

2 scoops vegan protein powder

1 cup strawberries

2 cups unsweetened coconut milk

Directions:

Add all ingredients into the blender and blend until smooth and creamy.

Serve immediately and enjoy.

Nutrition:

Calories: 221 Cal

Fat: 5.7 g

Carbs: 15 g

Protein: 27.7 g

161. Easy Chia Seed Pudding

Preparation Time: 10 Minutes

Cooking Time: 0

Servings: 4

Ingredients:

¼ tsp cinnamon

15 drops liquid stevia

½ tsp vanilla extract

½ cup chia seeds

2 cups unsweetened coconut milk

Directions:

Add all ingredients into the glass jar and mix well.

Close jar with lid and place in refrigerator for 4 hours.

Serve chilled and enjoy.

Nutrition:

Calories: 347 Cal

Fat: 33.2 g

Carbs: 9.8 g

Sugar: 4.1 g

Protein: 5.9 g

162. Grain-free Overnight Oats

Preparation Time: 10 Minutes

Cooking Time: 0

Servings: 1

Ingredients:

2/3 cup unsweetened coconut milk

2 tsp chia seeds

2 tbsp vanilla protein powder

½ tbsp coconut flour

3 tbsp hemp hearts

Directions:

Add all ingredients into the glass jar and stir to combine.

Close jar with lid and place in refrigerator for overnight.

Top with fresh berries and serve.

Nutrition:

Calories: 378 Cal

Fat: 22.5 g

Carbs: 15 g

Protein: 27 g

163. Avocado Tofu Scramble

Preparation Time: 15 Minutes

Cooking Time: 7 Minutes

Serves: 1

Ingredients:

1 tbsp fresh parsley, chopped

½ medium avocado

½ block firm tofu, drained and crumbled

½ cup bell pepper, chopped

½ cup onion, chopped

1 tsp olive oil

1 tbsp water

¼ tsp cumin

¼ tsp garlic powder

¼ tsp paprika

¼ tsp turmeric

1 tbsp nutritional yeast

Pepper

Salt

Directions:

In a small bowl, mix together nutritional yeast, water, and spices. Set aside.

Heat olive oil to the pan over medium heat.

Add onion and bell pepper and sauté for 5 minutes.

Add crumbled tofu and nutritional yeast to the pan and sauté for 2 minutes.

Top with parsley and avocado.

Serve and enjoy.

Nutrition:

Calories: 164 Cal

Fat: 9.7 g

Carbs: 15 g

Protein: 7.4 g

164. Cinnamon Coconut Pancake

Preparation Time: 15 Minutes

Cooking Time: 10 Minutes

Serves: 1

Ingredients:

1/2 cup almond milk

1/4 cup coconut flour

2 tbsp egg replacer

8 tbsp water

1 packet stevia

1/8 tsp cinnamon

1/2 tsp baking powder

1 tsp vanilla extract

1/8 tsp salt

Directions:

In a small bowl, mix together egg replacer and 8 tablespoons of water.

Add all ingredients into the mixing bowl and stir until combined.

Spray pan with cooking spray and heat over medium heat.

Pour the desired amount of batter onto hot pan and cook until lightly golden brown.

Flip pancake and cook for a few minutes more.

Serve and enjoy.

Nutrition:

Calories: 110

Fat: 4.3 g

Carbs: 10.9 g

Protein: 7 g

165. Zucchini Muffins

Preparation Time: 10 Minutes

Cooking Time: 30 Minutes

Servings: 8

Ingredients:

1 cup almond flour

1 zucchini, grated

1/4 cup coconut oil, melted

15 drops liquid stevia

1/2 tsp baking soda

1/2 cup coconut flour

1/2 cup walnut, chopped

1 1/2 tsp cinnamon

3/4 cup unsweetened applesauce

1/8 tsp salt

Directions:

Preheat the oven to 325 F/ 162 C.

Spray muffin tray with cooking spray and set aside.

In a bowl, combine together grated zucchini, coconut oil, and stevia.

In another bowl, mix together coconut flour, baking soda, almond flour, walnut, cinnamon, and salt.

Add zucchini mixture into the coconut flour mixture and mix well.

Add applesauce and stir until well combined.

Pour batter into the prepared muffin tray and bake in preheated oven for 25-30 minutes.

Serve and enjoy.

Nutrition:

Calories 229

Fat 18.9 g

Carbs 12.5 g

Protein 5.2 g

Main Dishes Recipes

166. Creamy Brussels Sprouts Bowls

Preparation Time: 10 Minutes

Cooking Time: 30 Minutes

Servings: 4

Ingredients: 1 tablespoon olive oil

1-pound Brussels sprouts, trimmed and halved

1 cup coconut cream

½ teaspoon chili powder

½ teaspoon garam masala

½ teaspoon garlic powder

A pinch of salt and black pepper

1 tablespoon lime juice

Directions: In a roasting pan, combine the sprouts with the cream, chili powder and the other ingredients, toss, introduce in the oven at 380 degrees F and bake for 30 minutes.

Divide into bowls and serve for lunch.

Nutrition:

Calories: 219 Cal Fat: 18.3 g Fiber: 5.7 g

Carbs: 14.1 gProtein: 5.4 g

167. Green Beans and Radishes Bake

Preparation Time: 10 Minutes

Cooking Time: 25 Minutes

Servings: 4

Ingredients: 2 tablespoons olive oil

1-pound green beans, trimmed and halved

2 cups radishes, sliced   1 cup coconut cream

1 teaspoon sweet paprika

1 cup cashew cheese, shredded

Salt and black pepper to the taste

1 tablespoon chives, chopped

Directions:

In a roasting pan, combine the green beans with the radishes and the other ingredients except the cheese and toss. Sprinkle the cheese on top, introduce in the oven at 375 degrees F and bake for 25 minutes. Divide the mix between plates and serve.

Nutrition: Calories: 130 Cal Fat: 1 g Fiber: 0.4 g Carbs: 1 g Protein: 0.1 g

168.   Green Goddess Buddha Bowl

Preparation Time: 10 Minutes

Cooking Time: 5 Minutes

Servings: 1

Ingredients: 2 cups fresh spinach

2 tablespoons avocado oil

4 broccolini spears ⅛ teaspoon salt

⅛ teaspoon freshly ground black pepper

⅓ cup frozen cauliflower rice, thawed

2 tablespoons shredded carrots

½ avocado, sliced

1 tablespoon almond butter, melted

1 tablespoon minced fresh cilantro

Directions:

Place the spinach in the bottom of a medium serving bowl. In a skillet over medium-high heat, heat the avocado oil. Add the broccolini and sauté for 2 to 3 minutes. Season with the salt and pepper and transfer it to the bowl containing the spinach. Add the cauliflower rice to the skillet and cook for 3 minutes. Add it to the serving bowl. Top with the carrots and avocado. Drizzle with the melted almond butter, sprinkle the cilantro on top, and serve.

Nutrition:

Calories: 571 Cal Fat: 51 g Protein: 9 g

Carbs: 19 gFiber: 11 g

169.   Zucchini Sage Pasta

Preparation Time: 10 Minutes

Cooking Time: 5 Minutes

Servings: 1

Ingredients:

1 tablespoon grass-fed butter

1 tablespoon dried sage

¼ teaspoon ground nutmeg

1 zucchini, spiralized

2 ounces tofu, chopped

1 cup fresh spinach leaves

½ cup grated Parmesan cheese

Directions:

In a skillet over medium-high heat, melt the butter.

Add the sage and nutmeg and stir until fragrant, 1 to 2 minutes.

Stir in the zucchini and tofu, and cook, stirring, for 3 to 4 minutes.

Next, add the spinach and cook for an additional minute until the spinach wilts.

Remove from the heat and top with the Parmesan cheese.

Serve warm.

Nutrition:

Calories: 399 Cal

Fat: 27 g

Protein: 27 g

Carbs: 12 g

Fiber: 4 g

170. Broccoli Stir-Fry

Preparation Time: 5 Minutes

Cooking Time: 10 Minutes

Servings: 1

Ingredients:

1 cup fresh spinach

1 tablespoon coconut oil

½ cup broccoli florets

1 cup frozen cauliflower rice

2 ounces seitan strips or cubes

1 tablespoon toasted sesame oil

1 tablespoon soy sauce

½ avocado, sliced

Directions:

In a dry, nonstick pan over medium heat, wilt the spinach leaves. Remove from the heat and transfer to a serving plate.

Turn the temperature up to medium high, and in the same skillet, melt the coconut oil. Add the broccoli and frozen cauliflower rice. Cook for 5 to 6 minutes or until tender.

Place the vegetables on the wilted spinach. Top with the seitan.

In a small bowl, mix together the sesame oil and soy sauce.

Pour the dressing over the seitan and vegetables. Top with the avocado slices and enjoy warm.

Nutrition:

Calories: 664 Cal

Fat: 44 g

Protein: 49 g

Carbs: 18 g

Fiber: 13 g

171. Kale and Cashew Stir-Fry

Preparation Time: 5 Minutes

Cooking Time: 5 Minutes

Servings: 1

Ingredients:

1 tablespoon coconut oil

1 cup frozen cauliflower rice (or pearls)

½ cup frozen stir-fry vegetables

1 cup destemmed and torn kale (small pieces)

3 tablespoons tamari sauce or low-sodium soy sauce

⅓ cup chopped cashews

Directions:

In a skillet over medium heat, melt the coconut oil. Add the cauliflower, stir-fry vegetables, and kale, and cook for 2 to 3 minutes, or until tender but still crisp.

Pour in the tamari and toss the vegetables until they are coated with the sauce.

Transfer the stir-fry to a serving dish, top with the cashews, and enjoy.

Nutrition:

Calories: 523 Cal Fat: 35 g

Protein: 18 g

Carbs: 34 g Fiber: 6 g

172. Tofu Green Bean Casserole

Preparation Time: 15 Minutes

Cooking Time: 25 Minutes

Servings: 1

Ingredients:

Nonstick cooking spray

1 cauliflower head, chopped into florets

2 tablespoons coconut oil

¼ cup chopped onion

14 ounces green beans, trimmed

1 tablespoon salt

¼ teaspoon freshly ground black pepper

¾ cup full-fat coconut milk

10 ounces tofu

2 cups grated Parmesan cheese

cup shredded mozzarella cheese

Preheat the oven to 250°F. Grease a 9-by-13-inch casserole dish with cooking spray.

Put the cauliflower florets in a microwave-safe dish. Add 1 to 2 tablespoons of water and cover the dish with plastic wrap. Microwave the cauliflower for 8 minutes, or until tender enough to mash.

While the cauliflower is cooking, heat a skillet over medium heat and melt the coconut oil. Add the onions and green beans, and cook until slightly tender and bright green.

Once the cauliflower is cooked, transfer it to a high-powered blender. Add the salt, pepper, and coconut milk. Pulse until creamy.

Spread the cauliflower mash in an even layer in the prepared casserole dish. Place the green beans on top of the mash, and then crumble the tofu on top.

Cover with the Parmesan and mozzarella cheeses.

Bake the casserole for 15 minutes. For a bubbly cheesy crust, broil the casserole uncovered under a low heat for 1 to 2 minutes.

Nutrition:

Calories: 297 Cal

Fat: 21 g

Protein: 18 g

Carbs: 9 g

Fiber: 3 g

173.   Creamy Stuffed Peppers

Preparation Time: 10 Minutes

Cooking Time: 15 Minutes

Servings: 2

Ingredients:

2 green bell peppers, halved and deseeded

1 tablespoon olive oil

¼ cup chopped onion

1 teaspoon minced garlic

1 cup fresh spinach

12 ounces full-fat ricotta cheese 1 large egg

1 teaspoon dried basil

8 tablespoons grated Parmesan cheese

Directions:

Preheat the oven to 350°F. Line a baking sheet with aluminum foil.

Place the bell peppers on the baking sheet, cut-side up, and bake for 10 minutes. Set aside.

While the peppers are baking, set a skillet over medium-high heat and pour in the olive oil. Add the onion, garlic, and spinach and sauté for 2 minutes, or until the spinach is wilted.

Transfer the mixture to a mixing bowl. Stir in the ricotta cheese, egg, and basil. Mix well.

Fill each pepper half with equal amounts of filling and top with 2 tablespoons of Parmesan cheese.

Return the peppers to the oven and bake for an additional 5 minutes. Remove and serve.

Nutrition:

Calories: 546 Fat: 38g

Protein: 33g Carbs: 18g Fiber: 3g

174. Zucchini Pizza Boats

Preparation Time: 10 Minutes

Cooking Time: 30 Minutes

Servings: 1

Ingredients:

1 medium zucchini, halved lengthwise and deseeded

2 tablespoons olive oil

2 garlic cloves, minced 1 cup fresh spinach

2 tablespoons low-sugar marinara sauce

8 ounces full-fat ricotta cheese

Directions:

Line a baking sheet with aluminum foil.

Place the zucchini, hollow-side up, on the prepared baking sheet.

In a small skillet over medium-high heat, warm the olive oil.

Add the garlic and stir for 1 to 2 minutes or until fragrant; then add the spinach and stir until it wilts.

Divide the spinach mixture evenly between the zucchini halves. Top evenly with the marinara sauce and ricotta cheese.

Bake for 20 to 25 minutes, or until the cheese is melted and the zucchini is tender.

Nutrition: Calories: 689 Cal Fat: 57 g

Protein: 28 g Carbs: 16 gFiber: 3 g

175. Vegan Coconut Curry

Preparation Time: 15 Minutes

Cooking Time: 30 Minutes

Servings: 4

Ingredients:

2 tablespoons olive oil

½ yellow onion, diced

3 garlic cloves, minced

½ tablespoon minced fresh ginger

1 teaspoon garam masala

1 teaspoon curry powder

1 teaspoon ground cumin

1 (14-ounce) can diced, no-sugar-added tomatoes

3 (14-ounce) cans full-fat coconut milk

1 cauliflower head, cut into florets

2 large zucchinis, diced

1 cup chopped cashews

Directions:

In a stockpot over medium-high heat, warm the olive oil. Add the onion and sauté for 2 to 3 minutes.

Stir in the garlic, ginger, garam masala, curry powder, cumin, and tomatoes. Cook for 2 minutes.

Pour in the coconut milk and bring the mixture to a low simmer. Reduce the heat to low and simmer for 5 minutes. Stir in the cauliflower and zucchini, and simmer for an additional 20 minutes.

Top with the chopped cashews and serve.

Nutrition:

Calories: 997 Cal

Fat: 89 g

Protein: 15 g

Carbs: 34 g

Fiber: 12 g

176.   Chiles Rellenos

Preparation Time: 15 Minutes

Cooking Time: 50 Minutes

Servings: 8

Ingredients:

Nonstick cooking spray

8 poblano chiles 1 tablespoon olive oil

½ onion, chopped 2 garlic cloves, minced

1 cup chopped button mushrooms

4 cups fresh spinach ½ cup sour cream

½ cup heavy (whipping) cream

16 ounces shredded pepper Jack cheese

Directions:

Preheat the oven to 450°F. Spray a baking dish with cooking spray.

Cut a slit down the length of each pepper and carefully scoop out and discard all the seeds and membranes. Cut another slit horizontally at the top of the peppers to make an opening for the filling.

Place the peppers in the prepared baking dish and cook for about 20 minutes, or until they start to blister. Remove and set aside.

While the peppers are in the oven, set a skillet over medium-high heat and pour in the olive oil. Add the onion, garlic, and mushrooms and cook until fragrant, 2 to 3 minutes. Add the spinach and cook until wilted, 4 to 5 minutes.

Transfer the mushroom mixture to a medium mixing bowl. Add the sour cream, heavy cream, and pepper Jack cheese, and stir until combined.

Remove the peppers from the oven and stuff each one with an equal amount of filling. Close with a toothpick.

Return the peppers to the oven for an additional 15 minutes, or until the cheese is melted. Serve warm.

Nutrition:

Calories: 341 Cal Fat: 29 g Protein: 16 g

Carbs: 4 g Fiber: 1 g

177. Broccoli and Cauliflower Rice Casserole

Preparation Time: 5 Minutes

Cooking Time: 10 Minutes

Servings: 4

Ingredients: 2 tablespoons grass-fed butter

1 garlic clove, minced

3 cups frozen cauliflower rice

1 cup frozen broccoli rice ½ teaspoon salt

¼ teaspoon freshly ground black pepper

1 cup grated sharp cheddar cheese

¼ cup cream cheese, at room temperature

1 to 2 tablespoons heavy (whipping) cream

Directions:

In a medium skillet over medium-low heat, melt the butter.Add the garlic and sauté for 2 minutes or until fragrant. Add the cauliflower rice, broccoli rice, salt, and pepper.

Cook the mixture for about 4 minutes, and then remove from the heat. Stir in the cheddar cheese and cream cheese and thin the mixture to your desired consistency with the heavy cream.

Serve warm.

Nutrition:

Calories: 270 Cal Fat: 22 g Protein: 11 g

Carbs: 7 gFiber: 3 g

178. Cauliflower Fried Rice

Preparation Time: 2 Minutes

Cooking Time: 10 Minutes

Servings: 2

Ingredients: 1 tablespoon avocado oil

4 cups frozen cauliflower rice

1 cup frozen peas and carrots blend

½ tablespoon minced fresh ginger

2 tablespoons tamari sauce

2 tablespoons sesame oil 2 large eggs, beaten

2 scallions, finely chopped

Directions:

In a medium skillet over medium-high heat, warm the avocado oil.

Add the cauliflower, peas and carrots, ginger, tamari sauce, and sesame oil. Cook until the vegetables are cooked thoroughly, 5 to 6 minutes.

Add the eggs and scramble them into the vegetables.

Divide the mixture between 2 serving dishes and top with the scallions before serving.

Nutrition:

Calories: 362 Cal Fat: 26 g Protein: 14 g

Carbs: 18 g Fiber: 8 g

179. Mexican Zucchini Hash

Preparation Time: 5 Minutes

Cooking Time: 10 Minutes

Servings: 4

Ingredients: 2 tablespoons avocado oil

½ onion, diced 2 garlic cloves, minced

4 large zucchinis, diced ½ teaspoon salt

¼ teaspoon freshly ground black pepper

1 teaspoon ground cumin

1 cup sliced button mushrooms

1 cup queso blanco cheese

2 avocados, diced

2 tablespoons chopped fresh cilantro

Directions:

In a large skillet over medium-high heat, warm the avocado oil. Add the onion, garlic, and zucchini, and season with the salt, pepper, and cumin. Stir to mix.

Add the mushrooms and sauté for 4 to 6 minutes, or until the vegetables are soft.

Remove from the heat and top with the queso blanco, diced avocado, and cilantro. Serve warm.

Nutrition:

Calories: 401 Cal Fat: 29 g

Protein: 12 g Carbs: 23 gFiber: 10 g

180. Eggplant Lasagna

Preparation Time: 10 Minutes

Cooking Time: 1 Hour 10 Minutes

Servings: 4

Ingredients:

Nonstick cooking spray

1 large eggplant, cut into ⅛-inch-thick slices

Salt

1½ cups full-fat ricotta cheese

1 large egg

1 (28-ounce) can whole tomatoes, drained

1 cup grated Parmesan cheese

2 cups shredded mozzarella cheese

2 tablespoons dried parsley

Directions:

Preheat the oven to 375°F. Grease an 8-by-8-inch baking dish with cooking spray.

Sprinkle the eggplant slices with salt. Allow them to sit for 15 minutes and then blot with a paper towel.

In a dry skillet over high heat, cook the eggplant slices for 3 minutes on each side. Remove and set aside.

In a medium bowl, combine the ricotta cheese and egg, and stir well. Set aside.

Crush a handful of tomatoes and place them in the bottom of the prepared baking dish.

Layer a few slices of eggplant, a layer of cheese sauce, and another layer of crushed tomatoes. Repeat this layering until the dish is full.

Sprinkle the Parmesan and mozzarella cheeses on top, followed by the parsley.

Cover the dish with aluminum foil and bake for 40 minutes. Remove the foil and bake for an additional 10 minutes.

Remove the lasagna from the oven and let it sit for 5 minutes before cutting and serving.

Nutrition:

Calories: 439 Cal

Fat: 27g

Protein: 31g

Carbs: 18g

Fiber: 7g

181.   Spaghetti Squash Bake

Preparation Time: 10 Minutes

Cooking Time: 30 Minutes

Servings: 4

Ingredients:

Nonstick cooking spray

1 tablespoon grass-fed butter

5 garlic cloves, minced

½ cup water

1 teaspoon seasoned vegetable base

1 cup heavy (whipping) cream

4 cups cooked and shredded spaghetti squash

½ cup grated Parmesan cheese

½ cup shredded mozzarella cheese

2 tablespoons chopped fresh parsley

1 teaspoon freshly ground black pepper

Directions:

Preheat the oven to 350°F. Spray an 8-by-8-inch glass casserole dish with cooking spray.

In a medium saucepan over medium-low heat, melt the butter. Add the garlic and cook until fragrant, 2 to 3 minutes.

Add the water, vegetable base, and cream. Cook until well combined, and then remove from the heat.

Place the squash in the bottom of the prepared dish. Pour the cream mixture on top, and then top with the Parmesan and mozzarella cheeses, parsley, and pepper.

Bake for 20 minutes and serve warm.

Nutrition:

Calories: 371 Cal Fat: 31g

Protein: 11g Carbs: 12g

Fiber: 1g

182. Cheesy Spinach Bake

Preparation Time: 10 Minutes

Cooking Time: 40 Minutes

Servings: 4

Ingredients:

Nonstick cooking spray

2 tablespoons grass-fed butter

2 cups chopped onion

2 garlic cloves, minced

2 zucchinis, chopped into bite-size pieces

2 cups fresh spinach

3 eggs, beaten

¼ cup heavy (whipping) cream

½ teaspoon salt

¼ teaspoon freshly ground black pepper

1½ cups shredded mozzarella cheese

½ cup grated Parmesan cheese

Directions:

Preheat the oven to 350°F. Coat a 9-inch glass pie plate with cooking spray.

In a skillet over medium-high heat, melt the butter. Add the onion and garlic and sauté for 2 minutes.

Add the zucchini and cook for another 4 minutes. Add the spinach and stir until wilted.

Transfer the mixture to the prepared pie plate and spread it evenly with a spatula.

In a small bowl, mix together the eggs, cream, salt, and pepper. Pour the mixture over the vegetables.

Top with the mozzarella and Parmesan cheeses and bake for 30 to 35 minutes. Serve warm.

Nutrition:

Calories: 386 Cal

Fat: 30 g

Protein: 21 g

Carbs: 8g

Fiber: 2g

183. Fakeachini Alfredo

Preparation: Time: 15 Minutes

Cooking Time: 5 Minutes

Servings: 1

Ingredients:

½ tablespoon extra-virgin olive oil

1 teaspoon minced garlic

¼ teaspoon salt

¼ teaspoon garlic powder

1 wedge Laughing Cow Swiss cheese, cubed

1 to 2 tablespoons heavy (whipping) cream

3 tablespoons grated Parmesan cheese

2 ounces seitan strips or cubes

⅓ cup cooked spaghetti squash

1 tablespoon chopped fresh parsley

Directions:

In a small saucepan over medium-low heat, warm the olive oil. Add the garlic, salt, and garlic powder and stir for 1 to 2 minutes or until fragrant.

Add the cubed cheese and stir until melted. Thin the sauce to your desired consistency with the cream. Lower the heat and stir in the Parmesan cheese. Continue to stir until melted.

Add the seitan to the sauce.

Place the squash in a serving bowl, pour the sauce on top, and sprinkle with the parsley.

Nutrition:

Calories: 452 Cal

Fat: 24 g

Protein: 52 g

Carbs: 7 g

Fiber: 3 g

184. Cheesy Cauliflower Mac 'N' Cheese

Preparation Time: 10 Minutes

Cooking Time: 30 Minutes

Serving: 6

Ingredients:

Nonstick cooking spray

1 cauliflower head, chopped into small florets

8 ounces heavy (whipping) cream

4 ounces shredded sharp cheddar cheese

4 ounces grated Parmesan cheese

2 ounces cream cheese 1 teaspoon salt

¼ teaspoon freshly ground black pepper

Directions:

Preheat the oven to 375°F. Spray an 8-by-8-inch baking dish with cooking spray. Place the cauliflower in a microwave-safe bowl and cook for 3 minutes on high. Drain any excess liquid. In a small saucepan over medium heat, combine the heavy cream, cheddar cheese, Parmesan cheese, cream cheese, salt, and pepper. Stir until well combined, and then remove from the heat. Pour the cheese sauce over the cauliflower and toss to coat. Transfer the mixture to the prepared baking dish and cook for 25 minutes.

Nutrition: Calories: 324

Fat: 28g Protein: 13g Carbs: 5g Fiber: 1g

185. Margherita Pizza

Preparation Time: 10 Minutes

Cooking Time: 5 Minutes

Servings: 1

Ingredients:

1 tablespoon psyllium husk powder

¼ teaspoon salt

½ teaspoon dried oregano

2 large eggs

1 tablespoon avocado oil

3 tablespoons low-sugar marinara sauce

2 tablespoons grated Parmesan cheese

½ cup sliced mozzarella cheese

1 tablespoon chopped fresh basil

Directions:

Line a baking sheet with aluminum foil. Turn the oven to low broil.

Combine the psyllium husk powder, salt, oregano, and eggs in a blender. Blend for 30 seconds. Set aside.

In a sauté pan or skillet, over high heat, warm the avocado oil. Pour the crust mixture into the pan, spreading it out into a circle.

Cook until the edges are browned, then flip the crust and cook for an additional minute.

Transfer the crust to the prepared baking sheet. Spread the marinara sauce over the top and cover with the Parmesan and mozzarella cheeses.

Broil until the cheese is melted and bubbling.

Top with the basil and enjoy.

Nutrition:

Calories: 545 Cal

Fat: 41 g

Protein: 32 g

Carbs: 12 g

Fiber: 8 g

Soups and Stews Recipes

186. Creamy Onion Soup

Preparation Time: 10minutes

Cooking Time: 65 Minutes

Servings: 4

Ingredients:

3 tbsp olive oil

3 cups thinly sliced white onions

2 garlic cloves, thinly sliced

2 tsp almond flour

½ cup dry white wine

Salt and black pepper to taste

2 sprigs chopped thyme

2 cups hot vegetable broth

2 cups almond milk

1 cup grates Swiss cheese

Directions:

Heat the olive oil in a pot over medium heat. Sauté the onions for 10 minutes or until softened, stirring regularly to avoid browning. Reduce the heat to low and cook further for 15 minutes while occasionally stirring.

Mix in the garlic, cook further for 10 minutes or until the onions caramelize.

Stir in the almond flour well, wine, and increase the heat. Season with salt, black pepper, thyme, and pour in the hot vegetable broth. Cover the pot, bring to a boil, and then simmer for 30 minutes.

Pour in the almond milk and half of the Swiss cheese. Stir until the cheese melts, adjust the taste with salt, black pepper, and dish the soup.

Top with the remaining cheese and serve warm.

Nutrition:

Calories: 183 Cal

Fat: 14.7 g

Carbs: 8 g

Fiber: 2 g

Protein: 8 g

187. Lettuce and Cauliflower Soup

Preparation Time: 10 Minutes

Cooking Time: 30 Minutes

Servings: 4

Ingredients:

1 tbsp olive oil

2 tbsp butter

1 medium red onion, thinly sliced

3 garlic cloves, finely sliced

1 large head cauliflower, cut into florets

1 medium lettuce head, leaves extracted and chopped

4 cups vegetable stock

6 sprigs parsley, leaves extracted

Salt and black pepper to taste

1 tbsp fresh dill leaves for garnishing

1 cup grated provolone cheese for topping

Directions:

Heat the oil and butter in a large saucepan over medium heat and sauté the onion and garlic until softened and fragrant, 3 minutes.

Stir in the cauliflower, lettuce, and cook until the lettuce wilts, 3 minutes

Pour in the vegetable stock, parsley and season with salt and black pepper. Close the lid, bring to a boil, and then simmer until the cauliflower softens.

Open the lid and using an immersion blender, puree the soup until smooth. Adjust the taste with salt and black pepper.

Dish the soup, top with the provolone cheese, and serve warm.

Nutrition:

Calories: 312 Cal

Fat: 21 g

Carbs: 15 g

Fiber: 5 g

Protein: 19 g

188. Spring Vegetable Soup

Preparation Time: 8 Minutes

Cooking Time: 13 Minutes

Servings: 4

Ingredients:

4 cups vegetable stock

3 cups green beans, chopped

2 cups asparagus, chopped

1 cup pearl onions, peeled and halved

2 cups baby spinach

1 tbsp garlic powder

Salt and white pepper to taste

2 cups grated cheddar cheese for topping

Directions:

In a large pot, add the vegetable stock, green beans, asparagus, and pearl onions. Bring to a boil over medium heat and then simmer until the vegetables soften, 10 minutes.

Stir in the spinach, allow slight wilting, and adjust the taste with salt and white pepper.

Dish the soup, top with the cheddar cheese, and serve warm.

Nutrition:

Calories: 405 Cal

Fat: 32.2 g

Carbs: 18 g

Fiber:4 g

Protein: 16 g

189.   Creamy Garlicky Tofu Soup

Preparation Time: 10 Minutes

Cooking Time: 11 Minutes

Servings: 4

Ingredients:

1 tbsp olive oil

1 large white onion, finely chopped

3 tbsp minced garlic

1 tsp ginger puree

1 cup vegetable stock

2 parsnips, peeled and chopped

Salt and black pepper to taste

2 (14 oz) silken tofu, drained and rinsed

2 cups almond milk

1 tbsp chopped fresh basil

1 tbsp chopped fresh parsley to garnish

Chopped toasted pecans for topping

Directions:

Heat the olive oil in a saucepan and sauté the onion, garlic, and ginger puree until fragrant and soft, 3 minutes

Mix in the vegetable stock, parsnips, salt, and black pepper. Cover and cook until the parsnips soften, 6 minutes.

Add the silken tofu and immediately puree the soup using an immersion blender until very smooth.

Stir in the almond milk, basil, and cook further for 2 minutes with frequent stirring to prevent the tofu from curdling.

Dish the soup, garnish with the parsley, pecans, and serve warm.

Nutrition:

Calories:171 Cal Fat: 13.9 g Carbs: 12 g

Fiber: 6 gProtein: 3 g

190. Kale Ginger Soup with Avocados

Preparation Time: 8 Minutes

Cooking Time: 8 Minutes

Servings: 4

Ingredients:

1 tbsp butter

1 tbsp sesame oil + extra for drizzling

1 small onion, finely sliced

3 garlic cloves, minced

2 tsp ginger paste

2 cups baby kale, chopped

2 cups chopped green beans

4 cups vegetable stock

3 tbsp chopped fresh cilantro + extra for garnish

Salt and black pepper to taste

1 large avocado, pitted, peeled, and diced for topping

Directions:

Heat the butter and sesame oil in a large pot over medium heat.

Sauté the onions, garlic, and garlic until softened and fragrant, 3 minutes.

Mix in the kale, green beans, vegetable stock, and cilantro. Season with salt, black pepper, and cook covered until the vegetables soften, 5 minutes.

Open the lid, adjust the taste with salt, black pepper, and dish the soup.

Top with the avocado and serve warm.

Nutrition:

Calories: 212 Cal

Fat: 16.1 g

Carbs: 14 g

Fiber: 2 g

Protein: 5 g

191. Creamy Tomato & Turnip Soup

Preparation Time: 10 Minutes

Cooking Time: 18 Minutes

Servings: 4

Ingredients:

2 tbsp butter

1 large red onion, chopped

4 garlic cloves, minced

6 red bell peppers, deseeded and sliced

2 turnips, peeled and diced

3 cups chopped tomatoes

4 cups vegetable stock

Salt and black pepper to taste

1 cup heavy cream

½ cup grated Swiss cheese

2 cups toasted chopped cashew nuts

Directions:

Melt the butter in a large pot over medium heat and sauté the onion and garlic until softened and fragrant, 3 minutes.

Stir in the bell peppers, turnips, tomatoes, vegetable stock, and season with salt and black pepper.

Bring to a boil and then simmer until the turnips and very tender, 15 minutes.

Insert an immersion blender and puree the soup until smooth.

Mix in the heavy cream and adjust the taste with salt and black pepper.

Dish the soup, top with the Swiss cheese, cashew nuts, and serve warm.

Nutrition:

Calories: 486 Cal

Fat: 41.3 g

Carbs: 14 g

Fiber: 2 g

Protein: 17 g

192. Italian Cheese Soup

Preparation Time: 12 Minutes

Cooking Time: 20 Minutes

Servings: 4

Ingredients:

1 tbsp avocado oil

6 slices vegan bacon, chopped

4 tbsp butter

1 small white onion, roughly chopped

3 garlic cloves, minced

2 tbsp chopped fresh Italian mixed herbs

2 cups peeled and cubed rutabagas

3 ½ cups vegetable broth

Salt and black pepper to taste

1 cup almond milk

1 cup grated provolone

2 tbsp chopped scallions for garnishing

Directions:

Heat the olive oil in a medium pot over medium heat and cook the vegan bacon until brown and crispy, 5 minutes. Transfer to a plate and set aside.

Melt the butter in the pot and sauté the onion, garlic, and mixed herbs until fragrant, 3 minutes.

Stir in the rutabagas, season with salt, black pepper, and cook for 10 to 12 minutes or until the rutabagas soften.

Open the lid, insert an immersion blender, and process the soup until very smooth.

Stir in the almond milk and provolone cheese until the cheese melts.

Adjust the taste with salt, black pepper, and dish the soup into serving bowls.

Garnish with the scallions and serve warm.

Nutrition:

Calories: 646 Cal

Fat: 63.7g

Carbs: 24 g

Fiber: 13 g

Protein: 8 g

193. Chilled Lemongrass and Avocado Soup

Preparation Time: 5 Minutes

Cooking Time: 5 Minutes

Servings: 4

Ingredients:

4 cups chopped avocado pulp

2 stalks lemongrass, chopped

4 cups vegetable broth

2 lemons, juiced

3 tbsp chopped mint + extra to garnish

Salt and black pepper to taste

2 cups coconut cream

Directions:

Over low heat, bring the avocado, lemongrass, and vegetable broth to a slow boil until the avocado warms through, 3 to 5 minutes.

Add the remaining Ingredients and process until smooth using an immersion blender.

Adjust the taste with salt, black pepper, and dish the soup.

Nutrition:

Calories: 391 Cal

Fat: 37.3 g

Carbs: 13 g

Fiber: 5 g

Protein: 7 g

194.   Mixed Mushroom Soup

Preparation Time: 10minutes

Cooking Time: 29minutes

Servings: 4

Ingredients:

4 oz unsalted butter

1 small onion, finely chopped

1 clove garlic, minced

5 oz. white button mushrooms, chopped

5 oz. cremini mushrooms, chopped

5 oz. oyster mushrooms, chopped

½ lb. celery root, chopped

½ tsp dried rosemary

3 cups vegetable broth

1 tbsp plain vinegar

1 cup cashew cream

4 basil leaves, chopped

2 tbsp chopped blanched almonds

Directions:

Melt the butter in a medium pot and sauté the Ingredients up to the vegetable stock until softened, 5 minutes.

Mix in the vegetable broth, vinegar, and bring the food to a boil. Reduce the heat to low and simmer until the liquid reduces by one-third.

Mix in the cashew cream and puree the Ingredients using an immersion blender. Simmer for 2 minutes.

Dish the soup, garnish with the basil, almonds, and serve warm.

Nutrition:

Calories: 325 Cal

Fat: 30.6 g

Carbs: 11 g

Fiber: 2 g

Protein: 8 g

195.   Coconut Pumpkin Soup

Preparation Time: 8 Minutes

Cooking Time: 15 Minutes

Servings: 4

Ingredients:

2 tbsp + 2 tbsp butter

2 small red onions

2 garlic cloves

1 cup chopped pumpkins

2 cups vegetable broth

Salt and black pepper to taste

½ cup coconut cream

½ lemon, juiced

¾ cup mayonnaise

Pumpkin seeds for garnishing

Directions:

Melt 2 tbsp of butter in a medium pot and sauté the onion and garlic until softened and fragrant, 3 minutes.

Stir in the pumpkins, vegetable broth, salt, and black pepper. Close the lid, allow boiling, and then simmer for 10 minutes

Open the lid, add the remaining butter, coconut cream, and puree the soup with an immersion blender until smooth.

Mix in the lemon juice, mayonnaise, and adjust the taste with salt and black pepper.

Dish the soup, garnish with the pumpkin seeds, and serve warm.

Nutrition:

Calories: 566 Cal

Fat: 57.7 g

Carbs: 15 g

Fiber: 7 g

Protein: 6 g

196. Mushroom Bourguignon

Preparation Time: 10 Min

Cooking Time: 40 Min

Servings: 4

Ingredients:

2 tablespoons olive oil, isolated (see notes for without oil)

2 pounds mushrooms, cut (darker, crimini)

1 cup pearl onions, stripped and closes cut (defrosted whenever solidified)

1 huge carrot, diced

1 yellow onion, diced

1 piling teaspoon crisp thyme leaves or 1/2 teaspoon dried

mineral salt and broke pepper, to taste

2 or 3 cloves garlic, minced

1 cup full-bodied red wine

2 cups vegetable soup

2 tablespoons tomato glue

1 1/2 tablespoons flour

Directions

In a huge dutch broiler or substantial pot, heat 1 tablespoon oil over medium-high warmth, include mushrooms and pearl onions, burn until they start to take on a bit of shading, around 3 to 4 minutes.

Decrease warmth to medium, include the carrots, onions, garlic, thyme, salt, and pepper, saute for 5 to 7 minutes, blending once in a while, until onions are softly cooked.

Add the red wine slowly to the pot and scrape any bits that are adhered to the base or sides. Go warm to medium-high and decrease wine significantly.

Mix in tomato glue and juices, heat to the point of boiling, lessen warmth to low and stew for 20 minutes, or until mushrooms are delicate. Let stew, secured or spread aslant, blending at times, and appreciate the brilliant fragrance.

In a little bowl, combine the rest of the tablespoon oil, or water, with flour to make a glue, mix into the stew. Stew for 10 minutes. In the event that the sauce is excessively slight, come it down to the correct consistency—season to taste.

Nutrition:

Calories:167 Cal

Fat:.4 g

Carbohydrate: 21.6 g

Fiber: 3.3 g

Protein: 7.1 g

197. Brussels Sprouts Stew

Preparation Time: 15 Minutes

Cooking Time: 20 Minutes

Servings: 4

Ingredients

1 lb. Brussels sprouts 1 medium Onion

1 tbsp Coconut oil 1 tsp Mustard seed

2 tbsp Cilantro (fresh)

4 cloves Garlic

2 medium Tomatoes

½ tsp Turmeric ½ tsp Cayenne pepper

2 tsp Curry powder ½ cup Cashews

1¾ cup canned Coconut milk (unsweetened)

Dash of Salt

1 Lemon

Directions

Halve brussels sprouts.

Dice tomatoes.

Finely dice onion.

Peel and smash garlic cloves into almost a paste.

Chop cilantro.

Set aside. Heat half of the oil over medium heat in a wide saucepan and add mustard seeds.

When they sputter, add the cilantro leaves and garlic. Sauté for about a minute.

Add the onions and sauté for a minute until they begin to turn translucent.

Add the tomatoes and powdered spices-- the curry powder, cayenne and turmeric.

Sauté, stirring frequently, until the tomatoes release most of their liquid and get pulpy.

Add the cashews, Brussels sprouts and some salt to taste.

Cover the saucepan to let the

Brussels sprouts get tender, around 5-8 minutes.

Stir occasionally to make sure nothing's sticking to the bottom.

If necessary, add a couple of tablespoons of water to the pan.

Add half the coconut milk and let the sauce come to a simmer.

Check if the Brussels sprouts are tender by piercing one with a fork in the center.

Add the remaining coconut milk and just warm through without letting the stew boil.

Check salt and add more if needed. Serve hot, with a squeeze of fresh lemon when serving.

Nutrition:

Calories: 404 Cal Carbs: 9.1 g

Fat: 32.8 g Protein: 10.5 g

198.   One Pot Vegan Chili Mac

Preparation Time: 10 minutes

Cooking Time: 20 minutes

Servings:

Ingredients:

1 tablespoon of olive oil or 1/4 cup water

1 huge onion, diced (any shading)

4 cloves garlic, minced

1 – 2 peppers (ringer or poblano), seeds expelled and diced

1 bundle (8oz.) tempeh, disintegrated

1 – 2 tablespoons stew powder

1 teaspoon cumin

1 teaspoon oregano

1 teaspoon paprika (smoked or ordinary)

1 can (15oz.) red kidney beans, depleted and washed

1 can (15oz.) sweet corn, depleted or 1/2 cups new or solidified

1 can (28oz) diced tomatoes (fire-roasted pref.)

4 cups vegetable soup or water

1 bottle dull lager (Modelo Negra) or 1/2 cups water

12 oz. elbow pasta (or other little pasta), around 2 1/2 cups

salt and pepper, to taste

Discretionary embellishment

shredded vegan cheddar

sliced green onions

vegan cashew sharp cream

fresh hacked cilantro

Directions

Saute: In a huge dutch broiler or pot, heat the oil/water over medium warmth, saute the onion, garlic, peppers, and tempeh for 5 minutes.

Include the stew powder, cumin, paprika, oregano and salt, cook 1 moment, or until pleasant and fragrant.

Bubble and stew: Add the tomatoes, pasta, beans, corn, and pour the fluids over the top, give a decent mix.

Heat to the point of boiling, spread aslant, lessen warmth and stew at a delicate moving bubble for 10 minutes, or until pasta is delicate—season with salt and pepper.

Include a touch of cayenne powder for additional warmth in the event that you like.

Serve warm with discretionary fixings.

Nutrition:

Calories:390 Cal Fat: 4 g

Carbs: 71.5 g Fiber: 9.4 g

Protein: 19.8 g

199. Spicy Carrot Stew

Preparation Time: 10 Minutes

Cooking Time: 3 Hours

Servings: 6

Ingredients:

1-pound carrots, peeled and cut with a spiralizer

1 cup red onion, chopped

2 garlic cloves, minced

2 celery ribs, chopped

1 teaspoon coriander, ground

1 teaspoon cumin, ground

½ teaspoon turmeric, ground

A pinch of cinnamon powder

Salt and black pepper to the taste

1 cup water 4 cups veggie stock

1 cup lentils

15 ounces canned tomatoes, chopped

1 tablespoon tomato paste

¼ cup cilantro, chopped

1 tablespoon spicy red pepper sauce

1 tablespoon lemon juice

Directions:

In your slow cooker, mix carrots with onion, garlic, celery, coriander, cumin, turmeric, cinnamon, salt, pepper, water, stock, lentils, tomatoes, tomato paste and pepper sauce, stir, cover and cook on High for 3 hours.

Add lemon juice and cilantro, stir, divide into bowls and serve.

Enjoy!

Nutrition:

Calories: 218 Cal

Fat: 4 g

Fiber: 4 g

Carbs: 8 g

Protein: 3 g

200. Mediterranean Stew

Preparation Time: 10 Minutes

Cooking Time: 7 Hours

Servings: 10

Ingredients:

2 cups eggplant, cubed

1 butternut squash, peeled and cubed

2 cups zucchini, cubed

10 ounces tomato sauce

1 carrot, sliced

1 yellow onion, chopped

½ cup veggie stock

10 ounces okra

1/3 cup raisins

2 garlic cloves, minced

½ teaspoon turmeric powder

½ teaspoon cumin, ground

½ teaspoon red pepper flakes, crushed

¼ teaspoon sweet paprika

¼ teaspoon cinnamon powder

Directions:

In your slow cooker, mix eggplant with squash, zucchini, tomato sauce, carrot, onion, okra, garlic, stock, raisins, turmeric, cumin, pepper flakes, paprika and cinnamon, stir, cover and cook on Low for 7 hours.

Stir your stew one more time, divide into bowls and serve.

Enjoy!

Nutrition:

Calories: 100 Cal

Fat: 3 g

Fiber: 4 g

Carbs: 24 g

Protein: 3 g

201. White Beans Stew

Preparation Time: 10 Minutes

Cooking Time: 4 Hours

Servings: 10

Ingredients:

2 pounds white beans

3 celery stalks, chopped

2 carrots, chopped

1 bay leaf

1 yellow onion, chopped

3 garlic cloves, minced

1 teaspoon rosemary, dried

1 teaspoon oregano, dried

1 teaspoon thyme, dried

10 cups water

Salt and black pepper to the taste

28 ounces canned tomatoes, chopped

6 cups chard, chopped

Directions:

In your slow cooker, mix white beans with celery, carrots, bay leaf, onion, garlic, rosemary, oregano, thyme, water, salt, pepper, tomatoes and chard, toss, cover and cook on High for 4 hours.

Stir your stew one more time, divide into bowls and serve.

Enjoy!

Nutrition:

Calories: 341 Cal

Fat: 8 g

Fiber: 12 g

Carbs: 20 g

Protein: 6 g

202. Vegetable Stew

Preparation Time: 25 Minutes

Cooking Time: 20 Minutes

Servings: 2-4

Ingredients

2 tbsp olive oil

1 turnip, chopped

1 onion, chopped

2 garlic cloves, pressed

½ cup celery, chopped

1 carrot, chopped

1 cup wild mushrooms, sliced

2 tbsp dry white wine

2 tbsp rosemary, chopped

1 thyme sprig, chopped

4 cups vegetable stock

½ tsp chili pepper

1 tsp smoked paprika 2 tomatoes, chopped

1 tbsp flax seed meal

Directions

Cook onion, carrot, celery, mushrooms, paprika, chili pepper, and garlic in warm oil over medium heat for 5-6 minutes until tender; set the vegetables aside.

Stir in wine to deglaze the stockpot's bottom. Place in thyme and rosemary. Pour in tomatoes, vegetable stock, reserved vegetables and turnip and allow to boil.

On low heat, allow the mixture to simmer for 15 minutes while covered. Stir in flax seed meal to thicken the stew. Plate into individual bowls and serve.

Nutrition:

Calories: 164 Cal Fat: 11.3 g

Carbs: 8.2 g Protein: 3.3 g

203. Italian Veggie Stew

Preparation Time: 20 Minutes

Cooking Time: 25 Minutes

Servings: 8

Ingredients:

2 tbsp. olive oil

1 minced celery stalk

½ minced medium yellow onion

2 minced garlic cloves

1 tsp Italian seasoning

½ tsp dried sage

½ tsp dried rosemary

10-ounce chopped Portobello mushrooms

10-ounce white button mushrooms

3¾ cups homemade vegetable broth

3 peeled and chopped medium carrots

3 cups chopped green beans

1 -15-ouncecan sugar-free diced tomatoes

1 -8-ouncecan sugar-free tomato sauce

1 tbsp. fresh lemon juice

Salt and freshly ground black pepper, to taste

2 tbsp. arrowroot starch

3 tbsp. water

Directions:

Place the coconut oil in the Instant Pot and select "Sauté". Then add the celery, onion and garlic for about 4-5 minutes.

Add Italian seasoning and herbs and cook for about 1 minute.

Add mushrooms and cook for about 4-5 minutes.

Select the "Cancel" and stir in remaining ingredients except for arrowroot starch and water.

Secure the lid and place the pressure valve to "Seal" position.

Select "Manual" and cook under "High Pressure" for about 15 minutes.

Select the "Cancel" and carefully do a "Natural" release.

Meanwhile in a small bowl dissolve arrowroot starch in water.

Remove the lid and select "Sauté".

Stir in arrowroot starch mixture and cook for about 2-3 minutes.

Select the "Cancel" and serve hot.

Nutrition:

Calories: 116 Cal

Fat: 4.7g Carbs: 1.75g

Pro tein: 6.6g

Fiber :4.1g

204.   Tofu & Veggies Stew

Preparation Time: 15 Minutes

Cooking Time: 30 Minutes

Servings: 6

Ingredients 2 tablespoons garlic, peeled

1 jalapeño pepper, seeded and chopped

1 -16-ounces jar roasted red peppers, rinsed, drained and chopped

2 cups vegetable broth 2 cups water

1 medium green bell pepper, seeded and thinly sliced

1 medium red bell pepper, seeded and thinly sliced

1 -16-ounces package extra-firm tofu, drained and cubed

1 -10-ounces package frozen baby spinach, thawed

Directions

Place the garlic, jalapeño pepper and roasted red peppers in a food processor and pulse until smooth.

In a large pan, add the peppers puree, broth, and water over medium-high heat and bring to a boil.

Add the bell peppers, and tofu and stir to combine.

Reduce the heat to medium and cook for about 5 minutes.

Stir in the spinach and cook for about 5 minutes.

Serve hot.

Nutrition:

Calories: 125 Cal Carbs: 7.5 g

Fiber: 3.5 g Protein: 11.7 g Fat: 5.3g

205. Lime Berries Stew

Preparation Time: 10 Minutes

Cooking Time: 20 Minutes

Servings: 6

Ingredients:

Zest of 1 lime, grated

Juice of 1 lime

1-pint strawberries, halved

2 cups water

2 tablespoons stevia

Directions:

In a pan, combine the strawberries with the lime juice, the water and stevia, toss, bring to a simmer and cook over medium heat for 20 minutes.

Divide the stew into bowls and serve cold.

Nutrition:

Calories: 172 Cal

Fat: 7 g

Fiber: 3.4 g

Carbs: 8 g

Protein: 2.3 g

Side Dishes Recipes

206. Basil Zucchinis and Eggplants

Preparation Time: 10 Minutes

Cooking Time: 20 Minutes

Servings: 4

Ingredients: 1 tablespoon olive oil

2 zucchinis, sliced   1 eggplant, roughly cubed

2 scallions, chopped

1 tablespoon sweet paprika

Juice of 1 lime

1 teaspoon fennel seeds, crushed

Salt and black pepper to the taste

1 tablespoon basil, chopped

Directions:

Heat up a pan with the oil over medium heat, add the scallions and fennel seeds and sauté for 5 minutes. Add zucchinis, eggplant and the other ingredients, toss, cook over medium heat for 15 minutes more, divide between plates and serve as a side dish.

Nutrition:

Calories: 97 Cal Fat: 4 g Fiber: 2 g

Carbs: 6 g Protein: 2 g

207. Chard and Peppers Mix

Preparation time: 10 minutes

Cooking time: 20 minutes

Servings: 4

Ingredients: 2 tablespoons avocado oil

2 spring onions, chopped   2 tablespoons tomato passata 2 tablespoons capers, drained

2 green bell peppers, cut into strips

1 teaspoon turmeric powder

A pinch of cayenne pepper Juice of 1 lime

Salt and black pepper to the taste

1 bunch red chard, torn

Directions: Heat up a pan with the oil over medium heat, add the spring onions, capers, turmeric and cayenne and sauté for 5 minutes. Add the peppers, chard and the other ingredients, toss, cook over medium heat for 15 minutes more, divide between plates and serve.

Nutrition: Calories: 119 Cal Fat: 7 g

Fiber: 3 g Carbs: 7 g Protein: 2 g

208. Balsamic Kale

Preparation time: 10 minutes

Cooking time: 20 minutes

Servings: 4

Ingredients:

1 tablespoon balsamic vinegar

2 tablespoons walnuts, chopped

1-pound kale, torn

1 tablespoon olive oil

1 teaspoon cumin, ground

1 teaspoon chili powder

3 garlic cloves, minced

2 tablespoons cilantro, chopped

Directions:

Heat up a pan with the oil over medium heat, add the garlic and the walnuts and cook for 2 minutes.

Add the kale, vinegar and the other ingredients, toss, cook over medium heat for 18 minutes more, divide between plates and serve as a side.

Nutrition:

Calories: 170 Cal Fat: 11 g

Fiber: 3 g

Carbs: 7 g Protein: 7 g

209. Mustard Cabbage Salad

Preparation Time: 10 Minutes

Cooking Time: 0

Servings: 4

Ingredients:

1 green cabbage head, shredded

1 red cabbage head, shredded

2 tablespoons avocado oil

2 tablespoons mustard

1 tablespoon balsamic vinegar

1 teaspoon hot paprika

Salt and black pepper to the taste

1 tablespoon dill, chopped

Directions:

In a bowl, mix the cabbage with the oil, mustard and the other ingredients, toss, divide between plates and serve as a side salad.

Nutrition:

Calories: 150 Cal

Fat: 3 g

Fiber: 2 g

Carbs: 2 g Protein: 7 g

210.   Cabbage and Green Beans

Preparation Time: 10 Minutes

Cooking Time: 15 Minutes

Servings: 4

Ingredients:

1 green cabbage head, shredded

2 cups green beans, trimmed and halved

2 tablespoons olive oil

1 teaspoon sweet paprika

1 teaspoon cumin, ground

Salt and black pepper to the taste

1 tablespoon chives, chopped

Directions:

Heat up a pan with the oil over medium heat, add the cabbage and the paprika and sauté for 2 minutes.

Add the green beans and the other ingredients, toss, cook over medium heat fro 13 minutes more, divide between plates and serve.

Nutrition:

Calories: 200 Cal

Fat: 4 g

Fiber: 2 g

Carbs: 3 g

Protein: 7 g

211.   Green Beans, Avocado and Scallions

Preparation Time: 10 Minutes

Cooking Time: 20 Minutes

Servings: 4

Ingredients:

1-pound green beans, trimmed and halved

1 avocado, peeled, pitted and sliced

4 scallions, chopped

2 tablespoons olive oil

1 tablespoon lime juice

Salt and black pepper to the taste

A handful cilantro, chopped

Directions:

Heat up a pan with the oil over medium heat, add the scallions and sauté for 2 minutes.

Add the green beans, lime juice and the other ingredients, toss, cook over medium heat for 18 minutes, divide between plates and serve.

Nutrition:

Calories: 200 Cal

Fat: 5 g

Fiber: 23 g

Carbs: 1 g

Protein: 3 g

212. Creamy Cajun Zucchinis

Preparation Time: 10 Minutes

Cooking Time: 20 Minutes

Servings: 4

Ingredients:

1-pound zucchinis, roughly cubed

2 tablespoons olive oil

4 scallions, chopped

Salt and black pepper to the taste

1 teaspoon Cajun seasoning

A pinch of cayenne pepper

1 cup coconut cream

1 tablespoon dill, chopped

Directions:

Heat up a pan with the oil over medium heat, add the scallions, cayenne and Cajun seasoning, stir and sauté for 5 minutes.

Add the zucchinis and the other ingredients, toss, cook over medium heat for 15 minutes more, divide between plates and serve.

Nutrition:

Calories: 200 Cal

Fat: 2 g

Fiber: 1 g

Carbs: 5 g

Protein: 8 g

213. Herbed Zucchinis and Olives

Preparation Time: 10 Minutes

Cooking Time: 20 Minutes

Servings: 4

Ingredients: 1 cup kalamata olives, pitted

1 cup green olives, pitted

1-pound zucchinis, roughly cubed

1 tablespoon rosemary, chopped

1 tablespoon basil, chopped

1 tablespoon cilantro, chopped

2 tablespoons olive oil 3 garlic cloves, minced

1 tablespoon lemon juice

1 teaspoon lemon zest, grated

1 tablespoon sweet paprika

A pinch of salt and black pepper

Directions:

Heat up a pan with the oil over medium heat, add the garlic, lemon zest and paprika and sauté for 2 minutes.

Add the olives, zucchinis and the other ingredients, toss, cook over medium heat for 18 minutes more, divide between plates and serve.

Nutrition:

Calories: 200 Cal Fat: 20 g Fiber: 4 g

Carbs: 3 g Protein: 1 g

214. Veggie Pan

Preparation Time: 10 Minutes

Cooking Time: 20 Minutes

Servings: 4

Ingredients:

1 cup green beans, trimmed and halved

1 cup cherry tomatoes, halved

1 zucchini, roughly cubed

1 red bell pepper, cut into strips

1 eggplant, cubed 3 scallions, chopped

2 tablespoons olive oil

2 tablespoons lime juice

Salt and black pepper to the taste

1 teaspoon chili powder

1 tablespoon cilantro, chopped

3 garlic cloves, minced

Directions:

Heat up a pan with the oil over medium heat, add the scallions, chili powder and the garlic and sauté for 5 minutes. Add the green beans, tomatoes and the other ingredients, toss, cook over medium heat for 15 minutes. Divide the mix between plates and serve as a side dish.

Nutrition:

Calories: 137 Cal Fat: 7.7 g

Fiber: 7.1 g Carbs: 18.1 g Protein: 3.4 g

215. Masala Brussels Sprouts

Preparation Time: 10 Minutes

Cooking Time: 35 Minutes

Servings: 4

Ingredients:

1-pound Brussels sprouts, trimmed and halved

Salt and black pepper to the taste

1 tablespoon garam masala

2 tablespoons olive oil

1 tablespoon caraway seeds

Directions:

In a roasting pan, combine the sprouts with the masala and the other ingredients, toss and bake at 400 degrees F for 35 minutes. Divide the mix between plates and serve.

Nutrition:

Calories: 115 Cal Fat: 7.6 g

Fiber: 4.9 g Carbs: 11.2 g Protein: 4.2 g

216. Nutmeg Green Beans

Preparation Time: 10 Minutes

Cooking Time: 30 Minutes

Servings: 4

Ingredients:

2 tablespoons olive oil

½ cup coconut cream

1-pound green beans, trimmed and halved

1 teaspoon nutmeg, ground

A pinch of salt and cayenne pepper

½ teaspoon onion powder

½ teaspoon garlic powder

2 tablespoons parsley, chopped

Directions:

Heat up a pan with the oil over medium heat, add the green beans, nutmeg and the other ingredients, toss, cook for 30 minutes, divide the mix between plates and serve.

Nutrition:

Calories: 100 Cal

Fat: 13 g

Fiber: 2.3 g

Carbs: 5.1 g

Protein: 2 g

217. Cauliflower and Chives Mash

Preparation Time: 10 Minutes

Cooking Time: 20 Minutes

Servings: 4

Ingredients:

2 pounds cauliflower florets

2 cups water

1 teaspoon thyme, dried

1 teaspoon cumin, dried

1 cup coconut cream

2 garlic cloves, minced

A pinch of salt and black pepper

Directions:

Put the cauliflower florets in a pot, add the water and the other ingredients except the cream, bring to a simmer and cook over medium heat for 20 minutes.

Drain the cauliflower, add the cream, mash everything with a potato masher, whisk well, divide between plates and serve.

Nutrition:

Calories: 200 Cal

Fat: 14.7 g

Fiber: 7.2 g

Carbs: 16.3 g

Protein: 6.1 g

218. Baked Artichokes and Green Beans

Preparation Time: 10 Minutes

Cooking Time: 40 Minutes

Servings: 4

Ingredients:

1-pound green beans, trimmed and halved

3 scallions, chopped   2 tablespoons olive oil

1 cup canned artichoke hearts, drained and quartered

2 garlic cloves, minced

1/3 cup tomato passata

A pinch of salt and black pepper

2 teaspoons mustard powder

1 teaspoon cumin, ground

1 teaspoon coriander, ground

Directions:

Heat up a pan with the oil over medium heat, add the scallions and the garlic and sauté for 5 minutes. Add the green beans and the other ingredients, toss, introduce in the oven and bake at 390 degrees F for 35 minutes.

Divide the mix between plates and serve as a side dish.

Nutrition:

Calories: 132 Cal Fat: 7.8 g

Fiber: 6.9 g Carbs: 14.8 g Protein: 4.4 g

219. Cumin Cauliflower Rice and Broccoli

Preparation Time: 10 Minutes

Cooking Time: 25 Minutes

Servings: 4

Ingredients:

2 cups cauliflower rice

1 cup broccoli florets

2 tablespoons olive oil

4 scallions, chopped

1 teaspoon sweet paprika

1 teaspoon chili powder

1 cup vegetable stock

1 teaspoon red pepper flakes

A pinch of salt and black pepper

¼ teaspoon cumin, ground

Directions:

Heat up a pan with the oil over medium heat, add the scallions, paprika and chili powder and sauté for 5 minutes.

Add the cauliflower rice and the other ingredients, toss, bring to a simmer, cook over medium heat for 20 minutes, divide between plates and serve.

Nutrition: calories 81, fat 7.9, fiber 1.5, carbs 4.1, protein 1.1

220. Turmeric Cauliflower Rice and Tomatoes

Preparation Time: 10 Minutes

Cooking Time: 25 Minutes

Servings: 4

Ingredients: 2 tablespoons olive oil

2 cups cauliflower rice

2 scallions, chopped 2 garlic cloves, minced

1 cup cherry tomatoes, halved

1 teaspoon basil, dried

1 teaspoon oregano, dried

A pinch of salt and black pepper

¼ teaspoon turmeric powder

1 cup vegetable stock

A handful cilantro, chopped

Directions:

Heat up a pan with the oil over medium heat, add the scallions, garlic, basil, oregano and turmeric and sauté for 5 minutes.

Add the cauliflower rice, tomatoes and the remaining ingredients, toss, cook over medium heat for 20 minutes, divide between plates and serve as a side dish.

Nutrition:

Calories: 77 g Fat: 7.7 g Fiber: 1 g

Carbs: 3.7 g Protein: 0.7 g

221. Flavored Tomato and Okra Mix

Preparation Time: 10 Minutes

Cooking Time: 30 Minutes

Servings: 6

Ingredients: 1 cup scallions, chopped

1-pound cherry tomatoes, halved

2 cups okra, sliced

2 tablespoons avocado oil

4 garlic cloves, chopped

2 teaspoons oregano, dried

A pinch of salt and black pepper

2 teaspoons cumin, ground

1 cup veggie stock

2 tablespoons tomato passata

Directions:

Heat up a pan with the oil over medium heat, add the scallions and the garlic and sauté for 5 minutes.

Add the tomatoes, the okra and the other ingredients, toss, cook over medium heat for 25 minutes, divide between plates and serve as a side dish.

Nutrition:

Calories: 84 Cal Fat: 2.1 g Fiber: 5.4 g

Carbs: 14.8 g Protein: 4 g

222. Roasted Artichokes and Sauce

Preparation Time: 10 Minutes

Cooking Time: 30 Minutes

Servings: 4

Ingredients:

2 big artichokes, trimmed and halved

2 tablespoons avocado oil

Juice of 1 lime

1 teaspoon turmeric powder

1 cup coconut cream

A pinch of salt and black pepper

½ teaspoon onion powder

¼ teaspoon sweet paprika

1 teaspoon cumin, ground

Directions:

In a roasting pan, combine the artichokes with the oil, the lime juice and the other ingredients, toss and bake at 390 degrees F for 30 minutes.

Divide the artichokes and sauce between plates and serve.

Nutrition:

Calories: 190

Fat: 6 Fiber: 8

Carbs: 10 Protein: 9

223. Zucchini Risotto

Preparation Time: 10 Minutes

Cooking Time: 30 Minutes

Servings: 4

Ingredients:

½ cup shallots, chopped

2 tablespoons olive oil

3 garlic cloves, minced

2 cups cauliflower rice

1 cup zucchinis, cubed

2 cups veggie stock

½ cup white mushrooms, chopped

½ teaspoon coriander, ground

A pinch of salt and black pepper

¼ teaspoon oregano, dried

2 tablespoons parsley, chopped

Directions:

Heat up a pan with the oil over medium heat, add the shallots, garlic, mushrooms, coriander and oregano, stir and sauté for 10 minutes.

Add the cauliflower rice and the other ingredients, toss, cook for 20 minutes more, divide between plates and serve.

Nutrition:

Calories: 231 Cal Fat: 5 g Fiber: 3 g

Carbs: 9 g Protein: 12 g

224. Cabbage and Rice

Preparation Time: 10 Minutes

Cooking Time: 30 Minutes

Servings: 4

Ingredients:

1 cup green cabbage, shredded

1 cup cauliflower rice

2 tablespoons olive oil

2 tablespoons tomato passata

2 spring onions, chopped

2 teaspoons balsamic vinegar

A pinch of salt and black pepper

2 teaspoons fennel seeds, crushed

1 teaspoon coriander, ground

Directions:

Heat up a pan with the oil over medium heat, add the spring onions, fennel and coriander, stir and cook for 5 minutes.

Add the cabbage, cauliflower rice and the other ingredients, toss, cook over medium heat for 25 minutes more, divide between plates and serve.

Nutrition:

Calories: 200 Cal Fat: 4 g

Fiber: 1 g Carbs: 8 g Protein: 5 g

225. Tomato Risotto

Preparation Time: 10 Minutes

Cooking Time: 30 Minutes

Servings: 4

Ingredients:

1 cup shallots, chopped

2 cups cauliflower rice

3 tablespoons olive oil

2 cups veggie stock

1 cup tomatoes, crushed

¼ cup cilantro, chopped

½ teaspoon chili powder

1 teaspoon cumin, ground

1 teaspoon coriander, ground

Directions:

Heat up a pan with the oil over medium heat, add the shallots and sauté for 5 minutes.

Add the cauliflower rice, tomatoes and the other ingredients, toss, cook over medium heat for 25 minutes more, divide between plates and serve.

Nutrition:

Calories 200 Cal

Fat 4 g

Fiber 3 g

Carbs 6 g

Protein 8 g

Snack Recipes

226.   Chipotle Tacos

Preparation Time: 10 Minutes

Cooking Time: 4 Hours

Servings: 4

Ingredients:

30 ounces canned pinto beans, drained

¾ cup chili sauce

3 ounces chipotle pepper in adobo sauce, chopped

1 cup corn

6 ounces tomato paste

1 tablespoon cocoa powder

½ teaspoon cinnamon, ground

1 teaspoon cumin, ground

8 vegan taco shells

Chopped avocado, for serving

Directions:

Put the beans in your slow cooker.

Add chili sauce, chipotle pepper, corn, tomato paste, cocoa powder, cinnamon and cumin.

Stir, cover and cook on Low for 4 hours. Divide beans and chopped avocado into taco shells and serve them.

Enjoy!

Nutrition:

Calories: 342

Fat: 3

Fiber: 6

Carbs: 12g

Protein: 10 g

227.   Tasty Spinach Dip

Preparation Time: 10 Minutes

Cooking Time: 4 Hours

Servings: 12

Ingredients:

8 ounces baby spinach

1 small yellow onion, chopped

8 ounces vegan cashew mozzarella, shredded

8 ounces tofu, cubed

1 cup vegan cashew parmesan cheese, grated

1 tablespoon garlic, minced

A pinch of cayenne pepper

A pinch of sea salt

Black pepper to the taste

Directions:

Put spinach in your slow cooker.

Add onion, cashew mozzarella, tofu, cashew parmesan, salt, pepper, cayenne and garlic.

Stir, cover and cook on Low for 2 hours.

Stir your dip well, cover and cook on Low for 2 more hours.

Divide your spinach dip into bowls and serve.

Enjoy!

Nutrition:

Calories: 200 Cal

Fat: 3 g

Fiber: 4 g

Carbs: 6 g

Protein: 8 g

228. Candied Almonds

Preparation time: 10 minutes

Cooking time: 4 hours

Servings: 10

Ingredients:

3 tablespoons cinnamon powder

3 cups palm sugar

4 and ½ cups almonds, raw

¼ cup water

2 teaspoons vanilla extract

Directions:

In a bowl, mix water with vanilla extract and whisk.

In another bowl, mix cinnamon with sugar and stir.

Dip almonds in water, then add them to the bowl with the cinnamon sugar.

Toss to coat really well, add almonds to your slow cooker, cover and cook on Low for 4 hours, stirring often.

Divide into bowls and serve as a snack.

Enjoy!

Nutrition:

Calories: 150 Fat: 3

Fiber: 4 Carbs: 6

Protein: 8

229. Eggplant Tapenade

Preparation Time: 10 Minutes

Cooking Time: 7 Hours

Servings: 6

Ingredients:

1 and ½ cups tomatoes, chopped

3 cups eggplant, chopped

2 teaspoons capers

4 garlic cloves, minced

1 tablespoon basil, chopped

2 teaspoons balsamic vinegar

A pinch of sea salt

Black pepper to the taste

6 ounces green olives, pitted and sliced

Directions:

Put tomatoes and eggplant pieces in your slow cooker.

Add garlic, capers, basil and olives, stir, cover and cook on Low for 7 hours.

Add salt, pepper, vinegar, stir gently, divide into small bowls and serve as an appetizer.

Enjoy!

Nutrition:

Calories: 140 Cal Fat: 3 g Fiber: 5 g

Carbs: 7 g Protein: 5 g

230. Almond and Beans Fondue

Preparation Time: 10 Minutes

Cooking Time: 8 Hours

Servings: 4

Ingredients:

½ cup almonds

1 and ¼ cups water

1 teaspoon nutritional yeast flakes

¼ cup great northern beans

A pinch of sea salt

Black pepper to the taste

Baby carrots, steamed for serving

Tofu cubes for serving

Directions:

Put the water in your slow cooker.

Add almonds and beans, stir, cover and cook on Low for 8 hours.

Transfer these to your blender, add yeast flakes, a pinch of salt and black pepper and pulse really well.

Transfer to bowls and serve with baby carrots and tofu cubes on the side.

Enjoy!

Nutrition:

Calories: 200 Cal Fat: 4 g Fiber: 4 g

Carbs: 8 g Protein: 10 g

231. Beans in Rich Tomato Sauce

Preparation Time: 10 Minutes

Cooking Time: 8 Hours And 10 Minutes

Servings: 6

Ingredients:

1-pound lima beans, soaked for 6 hours and drained

2 celery ribs, chopped

2 tablespoons olive oil

2 onions, chopped

2 carrots, chopped

4 tablespoons tomato paste

3 garlic cloves, minced

A pinch of sea salt

Black pepper to the taste

7 cups water

1 bay l eaf

1 teaspoon oregano, dried

½ teaspoon thyme, dried

A pinch of red pepper, crushed

¼ cup parsley, chopped

1 cup cashew cheese, shredded

Directions:

Heat up a pan with the oil over medium high heat, add onions, stir and cook for 4 minutes.

Add garlic, celery, carrots, salt and pepper, stir, cook for 4-5 minutes more and transfer to your slow cooker.

Add beans, tomato paste, water, bay leaf, oregano, thyme and red pepper, stir, cover and cook on Low for 8 hours.

Add parsley, stir, divide into bowls and serve cold with cashew cheese on top.

Enjoy!

Nutrition:

Calories: 160 Cal

Fat: 3 g Fiber: 7 g Carbs: 9 g Protein: 12 g

232. Tasty Onion Dip

Preparation Time: 10 Minutes

Cooking Time: 8 Hours

Servings: 6

Ingredients:

3 cups yellow onions, chopped

A pinch of sea salt

2 tablespoons olive oil

1 tablespoon coconut butter

1 cup coconut milk

½ cup avocado mayonnaise

A pinch of cayenne pepper

Directions:

Put the onions in your slow cooker.

Add a pinch of salt, oil and coconut butter, stir well, cover and cook on High for 8 hours.

Drain excess liquid, transfer onion to a bowl, add coconut milk, avocado mayo and cayenne, stir really well and serve with potato chips on the side.

Enjoy!

Nutrition:

calories 200

fat 4

fiber 4

carbs 9

protein 7

233.   Special Beans Dip

Preparation Time: 10 Minutes

Cooking Time: 2 Hours

Servings: 20

Ingredients:

16 ounces canned beans, drained

1 cup mild hot sauce

2 cups cashew cheese, shredded

¾ cup coconut milk

¼ teaspoon cumin, ground

1 tablespoon chili powder

3 ounces tofu, cubed

Directions:

Put beans in your slow cooker.

Add hot sauce, cashew cheese, coconut milk, cumin, tofu and chili powder.

Stir, cover and cook for 2 hours.

Stir halfway.

Transfer to bowls and serve with corn chips on the side.

Enjoy!

Nutrition:

Calories 230

Fat 4

Fiber 6

Carbs 8

Protein 10

234.   Sweet and Spicy Nuts

Preparation Time: 10 Minutes

Cooking Time: 2 Hours

Servings: 20

Ingredients: 1 cup almonds, toasted

1 cup cashews

1 cup pecans, halved and toasted

1 cup hazelnuts, toasted and peeled

½ cup palm sugar 1 teaspoon ginger, grated

1/3 cup coconut butter, melted

½ teaspoon cinnamon powder

¼ teaspoon cloves, ground

A pinch of salt

A pinch of cayenne pepper

Directions:

Put almonds, pecans, cashews and hazelnuts in your slow cooker.

Add palm sugar, coconut butter, ginger, salt, cayenne, cloves and cinnamon.

Stir well, cover and cook on Low for 2 hours.

Divide into bowls and serve as a snack.

Enjoy!

Nutrition:

Calories: 110 Cal Fat: 3 g Fiber: 2 g

Carbs: 5 gProtein: 5g

235.   Delicious Corn Dip

Preparation Time: 10 Minutes

Cooking Time: 2 Hours And 15 Minutes

Servings: 8

Ingredients: 2 jalapenos, chopped

45 ounces canned corn kernels, drained

½ cup coconut milk

1 and ¼ cups cashew cheese, shredded

A pinch of sea salt

Black pepper to the taste

2 tablespoons chives, chopped

8 ounces tofu, cubed

Directions:

In your slow cooker, mix coconut milk with cashew cheese, corn, jalapenos, tofu, salt and pepper, stir, cover and cook on Low for 2 hours.

Stir your corn dip really well, cover slow cooker again and cook on High for 15 minutes.

Divide into bowls, sprinkle chives on top and serve as a vegan snack!

Enjoy!

Nutrition:

Calories 150 Fat 3

Fiber 2Carbs 8Protein 10

236. Roasted Almonds

Preparation Time: 5 Minutes

Cooking Time: 10 Minutes

Servings: 16

Ingredients:

2 cups whole almonds

1 tablespoon chili powder

½ teaspoon ground cinnamon

½ teaspoon ground cumin

½ teaspoon ground coriander

Salt and freshly ground black pepper, to taste

1 tablespoon olive oil

Directions:

Preheat the oven to 350 degrees F. Line a baking dish with a parchment paper.

In a bowl, add all ingredients and toss to coat well.

Transfer the almond mixture into the prepared baking dish in a single layer.

Roast for about 10 minutes, flipping twice in a middle way.

Remove from oven and keep aside to cool completely before serving.

You can preserve these roasted almonds in an airtight jar.

Nutrition:

Calories: 78 Cal

Fat: 6.9 g

Carbs: 2.9 g

Protein: 2.6 g

237. Cheese Biscuits

Preparation Time: 15 Minutes

Cooking Time: 15 Minutes

Servings: 8

Ingredients:

1/3 cup coconut flour, sifted

¼ teaspoon baking powder

Salt, to taste

4 organic eggs

¼ cup butter, melted and cooled

1 cup cheddar cheese, shredded

Directions:

Preheat the oven to 400 degrees F. Line a large cookie sheet with a greased piece of foil.

In a large bowl, mix together flour, baking powder, garlic powder, and salt.

In another bowl, add eggs and butter and beat well.

Add egg mixture into flour mixture and beat until well combined. Fold in cheese.

With a tablespoon, place the mixture onto prepared cookie sheets in a single layer.

Bake for about 15 minutes or until top becomes golden brown.

Nutrition: Calories: 142 Cal

Fat: 12.7 g   Carbs: 0.8 g   Protein: 8 g

238.   Baked Veggie Balls

Preparation Time: 15 Minutes

Cooking Time: 25 Minutes

Servings: 8

Ingredients:

2 medium sweet potatoes, peeled and cubed into ½-inch size

2 tablespoons unsweetened coconut milk

1 cup fresh kale leaves, trimmed and chopped

½ small yellow onion, chopped finely

1 teaspoon ground cumin

½ teaspoon granulated garlic

¼ teaspoon ground turmeric

Salt and freshly ground black pepper, to taste

¼ cup ground flax seeds

Directions:

Preheat the oven to 400 degrees F. Line a baking sheet with parchment paper.

In a pan of water, arrange a steamer basket.

Place the sweet potato in a steamer basket and steam for about 10-15 minutes.

In a large bowl, place the sweet potato and coconut milk and mash well.

Add remaining ingredients except for flax seeds and mix until well combined.

Make about 1½-2-inch balls from the mixture.

Arrange the balls onto the prepared baking sheet in a single layer and sprinkle with flax seeds.

Bake for about 20-25 minutes.

Nutrition:

Calories: 61 Cal

Fat: 2.1 g   Carbs: 9 g

Protein: 1.5 g

239. Celery Crackers

Preparation Time: 15 Minutes

Cooking Time: 2 Hours

Serves: 15

Ingredients:

10 celery stalks

1 teaspoon fresh rosemary leaves

1 teaspoon fresh thyme leaves

2 tablespoons raw apple cider vinegar

¼ cup avocado oil

Salt, to taste

3 cups flax seeds. Grounded roughly

Directions:

Preheat the oven to 225 degrees F. Line 2 large baking sheets with parchment paper.

In a food processor, add all ingredients except flax seeds and pulse until a puree forms.

Add flax seeds and pulse until well combined.

Transfer the dough into a bowl and keep aside for about 2-3 minutes.

Divide the dough into 2 portions.

Place 1 portion in each prepared baking sheets evenly.

With the back of a spatula, smooth and press the dough to ¼-inch thickness.

With a knife, score the squares in the dough.

Bake for about 2 hours, flipping once halfway through.

Remove from the oven and keep aside to cool on the baking sheet for about 15 minutes.

Nutrition:

Calories: 126 Cal

Fat: 7.6 g

Carbs: 7.1 g

Protein: 4.3 g

240. Deviled Eggs

Preparation Time: 10 minutes

Cooking time: 0

Servings: 12

Ingredients:

12 hard-boiled large organic eggs, peeled and sliced in half

½ cup mayonnaise

½ teaspoon salt

Cayenne pepper, to taste

Directions:

With a spoon, scoop out the egg yolks from each egg half and transfer into a large bowl.

With a fork, mash egg yolks slightly.

Add mayonnaise and salt and mix well.

Scoop the mayonnaise mixture in the egg halves evenly.

Serve with the sprinkling of cayenne pepper.

Nutrition:

Calories: 101 Cal Fat: 7.6 g

Carbs: 2.7 g Protein: 5.6 g

241.   Avocado Guacamole

Preparation Time: 10 Minutes

Cooking Time: 0

Servings: 4

Ingredients:

2 small ripe avocados, peeled, pitted and chopped

½ cup fresh cilantro leaves, chopped finely

1 tablespoon fresh lime juice

Pinch of freshly ground black pepper

Directions:

In a bowl, add all ingredients and with a fork, mash until well combined. Serve immediately.

Nutrition: Calories: 145 Cal Fat: 13.8 g

Carbohydrates: 6.2 g

Protein: 1.4 g

242.   Sweet Potato Fries

Preparation Time: 10 Minutes

Cooking Time: 25 Minutes

Servings: 3

Ingredients:

1 large sweet potato, peeled and cut into wedges

1 teaspoon ground turmeric

1 teaspoon ground cinnamon

Salt and freshly ground black pepper, to taste

1 tablespoon olive oil

Directions:

Preheat the oven to 425 degrees F. Line a baking sheet with a piece of foil.

In a large bowl, add all ingredients and toss to coat well.

Transfer the mixture onto the prepared baking sheet in a single layer.

Bake for about 25 minutes, flipping once after 15 minutes.

Nutrition:

Calories: 79 Cal

Fat: 37.3 g

Carbs: 8 g

Protein: 0 g

243. Kale Chips

Preparation Time: 10 Minutes

Cooking Time: 15 Minutes

Serving: 6

Ingredients:

1-pound fresh kale leaves, stemmed and torn

¼ teaspoon cayenne pepper

Salt, to taste

1 tablespoon olive oil

Directions:

Preheat the oven to 350 degrees F. Line a large baking sheet with a parchment paper.

Place kale pieces onto the prepared baking sheet in a single layer.

Sprinkle the kale with salt and drizzle with oil.

Bake for about 10-15 minutes.

Nutrition:

Calories: 57 Cal

Fat: 2.3 g

Carbs: 8 g

Protein: 2.3 g

244. Zucchini Sticks

Preparation Time: 10 Minutes

Cooking Time: 25 Minutes

Servings: 8

Ingredients:

2 zucchinis, cut into 3-inch sticks lengthwise

Salt, to taste 2 organic eggs

½ cup Parmesan cheese, grated

½ cup almonds, grounded

½ teaspoon Italian herb seasoning

Directions:

In a large colander, place zucchini sticks and sprinkle with salt. Keep aside for about 1 hour to drain. Preheat the oven to 425 degrees F. Line a large baking sheet with parchment paper. Squeeze the zucchini sticks to remove excess liquid. With a paper towel, pat dries the zucchini sticks. In a shallow dish, crack the eggs and beat. In another shallow dish, mix together remaining ingredients. Dip the zucchini sticks in egg and then coat with the cheese mixture evenly. Arrange the zucchini sticks into a prepared baking sheet in a single layer.

Bake for about 25 minutes, turning once halfway through.

Nutrition:

Calories: 133 Cal Fat: 9.2 g

Carbs: 4.5 g Protein: 9.4 g

245. Strawberry Gazpacho

Preparation Time: 15 minutes

Cooking Time: 0

Servings: 4

Ingredients:

3 large avocados, peeled, pitted and chopped

1/3 cup fresh cilantro leaves

3 cups homemade vegetable broth

2 tablespoons fresh lemon juice

1 teaspoon ground cumin

¼ teaspoon cayenne pepper

Salt, to taste

Directions:

In a blender, add all ingredients and pulse until smooth.

Transfer the gazpacho into a large bowl.

Cover and refrigerate to chill completely before serving.

Nutrition:

Calories: 227 Cal

Fat: 20.4 g

Carbs: 9 g

Pro tein: 4.5 g

Salad Recipes

246. Cherry Tomato Salad with Soy Chorizo

Preparation Time: 5 Minutes

Cooking Time: 5 Minutes

Servings: 4

Ingredients: 4 soy chorizos, chopped

2 ½ tbsp olive oil 2 tsp red wine vinegar

1 small red onion, finely chopped

2 ½ cups cherry tomatoes, halved

2 tbsp chopped cilantro

Salt and freshly ground black pepper to taste

3 tbsp sliced black olives to garnish

Directions:

Over medium fire, heat half tablespoon of olive oil in a skillet and fry soy chorizo until golden. Turn heat off. In a salad bowl, whisk remaining olive oil and vinegar. Add onion, cilantro, tomatoes, and soy chorizo. Mix with dressing and season with salt and black pepper. Garnish with olives and serve.

Nutrition: Calories: 138 Cal Fat: 8.95 g

Carbs: 5.63 g Fiber: 0.4 g Protein: 7.12 g

247. Roasted Bell Pepper Salad with Olives

Preparation Time: 10 Minutes

Cooking Time: 20 Minutes

Servings: 4

Ingredients:

8 large red bell peppers, deseeded and cut in wedges

½ tsp erythritol

2 ½ tbsp olive oil

1/3 cup arugula

1 tbsp mint leaves

1/3 cup pitted Kalamata olives

3 tbsp chopped almonds

½ tbsp balsamic vinegar

Crumbled feta cheese for topping

Toasted pine nuts for topping

Directions:

Preheat oven to 400o F.

Pour bell peppers on a roasting pan; season with erythritol and drizzle with half of olive oil. Roast in oven until slightly charred, 20 minutes. Remove from oven and set aside.

Arrange arugula in a salad bowl, scatter bell peppers on top, mint leaves, olives, almonds, and drizzle with balsamic vinegar and remaining olive oil. Season with salt and black pepper.

Toss; top with feta cheese and pine nuts and serve.

Nutrition:

Calories: 163 Cal

Fat: 13.3 g

Carbs: 6.53 g

Fiber: 2.2 g

Protein: 3.37 g

248. Tofu-Dulse-Walnut Salad

Preparation Time: 10 Minutes

Cooking Time: 15 Minutes

Servings: 4

Ingredients: 1 (7 oz) block extra firm tofu

2 tbsp olive oil 2 tbsp butter

1 cup asparagus, trimmed and halved

1 cup green beans, trimmed

2 tbsp chopped dulse

Salt and freshly ground black pepper to taste

½ lemon, juiced 4 tbsp chopped walnuts

Directions:

Place tofu in between two paper towels and allow soaking for 5 minutes. After, remove towels and chop into small cubes.

Heat olive oil in a skillet and fry tofu until golden, 10 minutes. Remove onto a paper towel-lined plate and set aside.

Melt butter in skillet and sauté asparagus and green beans until softened, 5 minutes. Add dulse, season with salt and black pepper, and cook until softened. Mix in tofu and stir-fry for 5 minutes. Plate, drizzle with lemon juice, and scatter walnuts on top.

Serve warm.

Nutrition: Calories 237 Fat 19.57g Carbs 5.9g

Fiber 2.1g Protein 12.75g

249. Almond-GojiBerry Cauliflower Salad

Preparation Time: 10 minutes

Cooking Time: 2 minutes

Servings: 4

Ingredients:

1 small head cauliflower, cut into florets

8 sun-dried tomatoes in olive oil, drained

12 pitted green olives, roughly chopped

1 lemon, zested and juiced

3 tbsp chopped green onions

A handful chopped almonds

¼ cup goji berries 1 tbsp sesame oil

½ cup watercress 3 tbsp chopped parsley

Salt and freshly ground black pepper to taste

Lemon wedges to garnish

Directions: Pour cauliflower into a large safe-microwave bowl, sprinkle with some water, and steam in microwave for 1 to 2 minutes or until softened. In a large salad bowl, combine cauliflower, tomatoes, olives, lemon zest and juice, green onions, almonds, goji berries, sesame oil, watercress, and parsley. Season with salt and black pepper, and mix well. Serve with lemon wedges.

Nutrition: Calories 203 CalFat 15:.28 g

Carbs: 9.64 g Fiber: 3.2 gProtein: 6.67 g

250. Warm Mushroom and Orange Pepper Salad

Preparation Time: 10 Minutes

Cooking Time: 8 Minutes

Servings: 4

Ingredients: 2 tbsp avocado oil

1 cup mixed mushrooms, chopped

2 orange bell peppers, deseeded and finely sliced

1 garlic clove, minced 2 tbsp tamarind sauce

1 tsp maple (sugar-free) syrup

½ tsp hot sauce ½ tsp fresh ginger paste

Sesame seeds to garnish

Directions:

Over medium fire, heat half of avocado oil in a large skillet, sauté mushroom and bell peppers until slightly softened, 5 minutes.

In a small bowl, whisk garlic, tamarind sauce, maple syrup, hot sauce, and ginger paste. Add mixture to vegetables and stir-fry for 2 to 3 minutes.

Turn heat off and dish salad. Drizzle with remaining avocado oil and garnish with sesame seeds. Serve with grilled tofu.

Nutrition:

Calories: 289 Cal Fat: 26.71 g Carbs: 9 g

Fiber: 3.8 g Protein: 4.23 g

251. Broccoli, Kelp, and Feta Salad

Preparation Time: 15 Minutes

Cooking Time: 0

Servings: 4

Ingredients: 2 tbsp olive oil

1 tbsp white wine vinegar   2 tbsp chia seeds

Salt and freshly ground black pepper to taste

2 cups broccoli slaw

1 cup chopped kelp, thoroughly washed and steamed

1/3 cup chopped pecans

1/3 cup pumpkin seeds

1/3 cup blueberries

2/3 cup ricotta cheese

Directions:

In a small bowl, whisk olive oil, white wine vinegar, chia seeds, salt, and black pepper. Set aside.

In a large salad bowl, combine the broccoli slaw, kelp, pecans, pumpkin seeds, blueberries, and ricotta cheese.

Drizzle dressing on top, toss, and serve.

Nutrition:

Calories 397 Fat 3.87gCarbs 8.4g

Fiber 3.5gProtein 8.93g

252. Roasted Asparagus with Feta Cheese Salad

Preparation Time: 10 minutes

Cooking Time: 20 minutes

Serving Size: 4

Ingredients: ½ tsp dried oregano

1 lb. asparagus, trimmed and halved

2 tbsp olive oil ½ tsp dried basil

Salt and freshly ground black pepper to taste

½ tsp hemp seeds

1 tbsp maple (sugar-free) syrup ½ cup arugula

4 tbsp crumbled feta cheese 2 tbsp hazelnuts

1 lemon, cut into wedges

Directions:

Preheat oven to 350oF.

Pour asparagus on a baking tray, drizzle with olive oil, basil, oregano, salt, black pepper, and hemp seeds. Mix with your hands and roast in oven for 15 minutes.

Remove, drizzle with maple syrup, and continue cooking until slightly charred, 5 minutes.

Spread arugula in a salad bowl and top with asparagus. Scatter with feta cheese, hazelnuts, and serve with lemon wedges.

Nutrition: Calories: 146 Cal Fat: 12.87 g

Carbs: 5.07 g Fiber: 1.6 g Protein: 4.44 g

253. Fresh Veggie Salad

Preparation Time: 20 Minutes

Cooking Time: 0

Servings: 8

Ingredients:

For Dressing: 5 tablespoons olive oil

3 tablespoons fresh lemon juice

2 tablespoons fresh mint leaves, chopped finely

1 teaspoon Erythritol

Salt and freshly ground black pepper, to taste

For Salad:

2 cups cucumbers, peeled and sliced

2 cups tomatoes, sliced

1 cup black olives 6 cups lettuce

1 cup mozzarella cheese, cubed

Directions:

For dressing: in a bowl, add all ingredients and beat until well combined.

Cover and refrigerate to chill for about 1 hour.

For the salad: in a large serving bowl, add all ingredients and mix. Pour dressing over salad and toss to coat well. Serve immediately.

Nutrition:

Calories: 124 Cal Fat: 11.4 g

Carbs: 5.4 g Protein: 2 g

254. Strawberry Salad

Preparation Time: 15 Minutes

Cooking Time: 0

Servings: 4

Ingredients:

6 cups fresh baby greens

2 cups fresh strawberries, hulled and sliced

1 tablespoon fresh mint leaves

¼ cup olive oil

2 tablespoons fresh lemon juice

¼ teaspoon liquid stevia

1/8 teaspoon paprika

1/8 teaspoon garlic powder

Salt, to taste

Directions:

For the salad: in a large serving bowl, add greens, strawberries, and mint and mix.

For dressing: in a bowl, add remaining ingredients and beat until well combined.

Pour dressing over salad and toss to coat well.

Serve immediately.

Nutrition:

Calories: 141 Cal Fat: 14.7 g

Carbs: 1.8 g Protein: 2 g

255. Tex Mex Black Bean and Avocado Salad

Preparation Time: 15 Minutes

Cooking Time: 0

Servings: 2

Ingredients

14 oz. black beans, drained and rinsed

3 jars roasted red peppers, chopped

1 avocado, chopped

½ onion, chopped

1 red chili, chopped

1 lime, plus wedges to serve

olive oil

1 teaspoon cumin seeds

2 handfuls rocket

2 pitta breads, warmed

Directions:

Combine beans, peppers, avocado, onion and chili in a large mixing bowl.

Add lime juice, cumin seeds and mix well.

Serve the rocket on two plates with warm pittas and divide the bean mixture.

Nut rition:

Calories: 120 Cal Fat: 3 g

Fiber: 5 g Carbs: 3 gProtein: 5 g

256. Lentil Fattoush Salad

Preparation Time: 10 Minutes

Cooking Time: 42 Minutes

Servings: 2

Ingredients:

⅓ cup dry green lentils

1 whole wheat pita pocket, chopped into bite sized pieces

2 teaspoons olive oil

2 teaspoons zaatar

4 cups loosely packed arugula

2 stalks celery, chopped

1 carrot stick, chopped

¼ small hothouse cucumber, chopped

1 small radish, thinly sliced

¼ cup dates, chopped

2 tablespoons toasted sunflower seeds

For the maple Dijon vinaigrette:

2 tablespoons olive oil

2 tablespoons balsamic vinegar

1 tablespoon Dijon mustard

1 tablespoon maple syrup

Directions:

Place a small pot over medium heat. Add lentils and 2/3 cup water.

Bring it to a boil, lower the heat and bring it to a simmer for 35 minutes. Remove from the heat and drain excess liquid.

Preheat the oven to 425F. Line a baking sheet with parchment paper.

Mix pita pieces with olive oil and zaatar. Place on a baking sheet and bake for 7 minutes.

Mix arugula, lentils, veggies, dates, sunflower seeds and pita croutons.

Meanwhile in a separate bowl, mix the dressing ingredients and set aside.

Add the dressing and toss well before serving.

Nutrition:

Calories: 154 Cal

Fat: 8.4 g

Fiber: 4.4 g

Carbs: 4.3 g

Protein: 7.1 g

257. Sweet Potato Salad

Preparation: 10 Minutes

Cooking Time: 30 Minutes

Servings: 4

Ingredients:

2 sweet potatoes, peeled and cubed

1 tablespoon olive oil

½ teaspoon each of paprika, oregano and cayenne pepper

1 shallot, diced

2 spring onions, chopped

1 small bunch chives, chopped

3 tablespoons red wine vinegar

2 teaspoons olive oil

1 tablespoon pure maple syrup

salt and pepper

Directions:

Preheat the oven to 300F and prepare a baking sheet by lining it with parchment paper.

Place sweet potatoes in the baking sheet.

Drizzle some olive oil and spices, toss well and bake for 30 minutes.

In a separate bowl, mix shallots, scallions, chives, vinegar, olive oil and maple syrup.

Add baked sweet potatoes to the dressing.

Nutrition:

Calories: 162 Cal

Fat: 8.0 g Fiber: 2.3 g

Carbs: 6.3 g

Protein: 8.1 g

258. Lentil Salad with Spinach and Pomegranate

Preparation Time: 15 Minutes

Cooking Time: 0

Servings: 3

Ingredients

For the vegan lentil salad:

3 cups brown lentils, cooked

1 avocado, cut into slices

2-3 handfuls fresh spinach

½ cup walnuts, chopped

2 apples, chopped

1 pomegranate

For the tahini orange dressing:

3 tablespoons tahini

2 tablespoons olive oil

1 clove of garlic

6 tablespoons water

4 tablespoons orange juice

2 teaspoons orange zest

salt and pepper

Directions:

Prepare lentils according to package instructions.

Place pomegranate in a shallow bowl filled with water, cut in half and take out seeds, remove fibers floating on the water.

Process all dressing ingredients in a food processor. Process until smooth and set aside.

Place salad ingredients in a large bowl and mix well.

Drizzle dressing over salad before serving.

Nutrition: Calories: 104 Cal

Fat: 5 g Fiber: 4 g Carbs: 3.1 g

Protein: 7.1 g

259. Broccoli Salad Curry Dressing

Preparation Time: 30 Minutes

Cooking Time: 0

Servings: 6

Ingredients

½ cup plain, unsweetened vegan yogurt

¼ cup onion, chopped

2 heads broccoli florets, chopped

2 stalks celery, chopped

½ teaspoon curry powder

¼ teaspoon salt or to taste

2 tablespoons sunflower seeds

Directions:

Mix yoghurt, curry powder and salt.

Toss broccoli florets, celery onion and sunflower seeds.

Drizzle the dressing on top and put the salad in the fridge for 30 minutes.

Nutrition:

Calories: 153 Cal Fat: 4 g

Fiber: 3 g Carbs: 2 g

Protein: 9.1 g

260.   Ginger Avocado Kale Salad

Preparation Time: 15 Minutes

Cooking Time: 0

Servings: 4

Ingredie nts:

1 avocado, peeled and sliced

1 tbsp ginger, grated

1/2 lb kale, chopped

1/4 cup parsley, chopped

2 fresh scallions, chopped

Directions:

Add all ingredients into the mixing bowl and toss well.

Serve and enjoy.

Nutrition:

Calories: 139 Cal Fat: 9.9 g

Carbs: 12 g Protein: 3 g

261.   Refreshing Cucumber Salad

Preparation Time: 10 Minutes

Cooking Time: 0

Servings: 4

Ingredients: 1/3 cup cucumber basil ranch

1 cucumber, chopped

3 tomatoes, chopped

3 tbsp fresh herbs, chopped

½ onion, sliced

Directions:

Add all ingredients into the large mixing bowl and toss well.

Serve immediately and enjoy.

Nutrition:

Calories 84

Fat 3.4 g

Carbs 12.5 g

Protein 2 g

262. Cabbage Coconut Salad

Preparation Time: 15 Minutes

Cooking Time: 0

Servings: 4

Ingredients:

1/3 cup unsweetened desiccated coconut

½ medium head cabbage, shredded

2 tsp sesame seeds

¼ cup tamari sauce

¼ cup olive oil

1 fresh lemon juice

½ tsp cumin

½ tsp curry powder

½ tsp ginger powder

Directions:

Add all ingredients into the large mixing bowl and toss well.

Place salad bowl in refrigerator for 1 hour.

Serve and enjoy.

Nutrition:

Calories: 197 Cal

Fat: 16.6 g

Carbs : 11.4 g

Protein: 3.5 g

263. Avocado Cabbage Salad

Preparation Time: 20 Minutes

Cooking Time: 0

Servings: 4

Ingredients:

2 avocados, diced

4 cups cabbage, shredded

3 tbsp fresh parsley, chopped

2 tbsp apple cider vinegar

4 tbsp olive oil

1 cup cherry tomatoes, halved

1/2 tsp pepper

1 1/2 tsp sea salt

Directions:

Add cabbage, avocados, and tomatoes to a medium bowl and mix well.

In a small bowl, whisk together oil, parsley, vinegar, pepper, and salt.

Pour dressing over vegetables and mix well.

Serve and enjoy.

Nutrition:

Calories: 253

Fat: 21.6 g

Carbs: 14 g

Protein: 3.5 g

264. Turnip Salad

Preparation Time: 10 Minutes

Cooking Time: 0

Servings: 4

Ingredients:

4 white turnips, spiralized

1 lemon juice

4 dill sprigs, chopped

2 tbsp olive oil

1 1/2 tsp salt

Directions:

Season spiralized turnip with salt and gently massage with hands.

Add lemon juice and dill. Season with pepper and salt.

Drizzle with olive oil and combine everything well.

Serve immediately and enjoy.

Nutrition:

Calories: 49

Fat: 1.1 g

Carbohydrates: 9 g

Protein: 1.4 g

265. Brussels sprouts Salad

Preparation Time: 20 Minutes

Cooking Time: 0

Servings: 6

Ingredients:

1 ½ lbs Brussels sprouts, trimmed

¼ cup toasted hazelnuts, chopped

2 tsp Dijon mustard

1 ½ tbsp lemon juice

2 tbsp olive oil

Pepper

Salt

Directions:

In a small bowl, whisk together oil, mustard, lemon juice, pepper, and salt.

In a large bowl, combine together Brussels sprouts and hazelnuts.

Pour dressing over salad and toss well.

Serve immediately and enjoy.

Nutrition:

Calories: 111

Fat: 7.1 g

Carbs: 11 g

Protein: 4.4 g

Dessert Low Sugar Recipes

266. Coconut Fat Bombs

Preparation Time: 1 Hr. 5 Minutes

Cooking Time: 0

Servings: 4

Ingredients:

20 drops liquid stevia

1 c. coconut flakes, unsweetened

¾ c. coconut oil

1 can coconut milk

Directions:

In a big microwave-safe mixing bowl, add coconut oil and warm on low power for 20 seconds to melt.

Whisk in coconut milk and stevia into the oil.

Add coconut flakes; combine well.

Pour into candy molds or ice cube trays and freeze for 1 hour.

Serve and enjoy.

Nutrition:

Calories: 89.1 Cal Carbs: 0.87 g

Proteins: 0.33 g Fats: 9.7 g

267. Coconut Cupcakes

Preparation Time: 1 Hour. 5 Minutes

Cooking Time: 0

Servings: 18

Ingredients:

1 tbsp. vanilla

1 t. baking soda

1 c. erythritol

4 t. baking powder

1 ¼ c. coconut milk

¾ c. coconut flour

14 tbsp. arrowroot powder

2 c. almond meal

½ c. coconut oil

Whipped Cream:

1 t. vanilla

¼ c. erythritol

2 13.5 oz. cans full-fat coconut milk, refrigerated overnight

Directions:

Prepare a muffin tin with muffin liners and bring the oven to 350 heat setting.

In a big mixing bowl, add all the ingredients and beat on medium-high speed until it turns to a batter-like consistency. If too dry, add ¼ teaspoon of water at a time.

Fill the cupcake cups with the batter, three-quarters full. Bake for 20 minutes or until the cupcakes are firm.

Place in the refrigerator to cool.

While cupcakes are cooling, make the whipped cream.

Remove the coconut milk from the fridge and pour the clear coconut water from the milk.

In a big mixing bowl, add the vanilla and erythritol; beat until fluffy. Ice the cupcakes and serve. Serve and enjoy.

Nutrition:

Calories: 202 Cal Carbs: 15.6 g

Proteins: 3.3 g Fats: 15.8 g

268. Pumpkin Truffles

Preparation Time: 15 Minutes

Cooking Time: 0

Servings: 12

Ingredients:

1 t. cinnamon

2 tbsp. coconut sugar

3 tbsp. coconut flour

½ c. almond flour

1 t. pumpkin pie spice

¼ t. salt

½ t. vanilla extract

¼ c. maple syrup

1 c. pumpkin puree

Directions:

Bring a saucepan to medium heat and add pumpkin puree, syrup, salt, and pumpkin pie spice, stirring constantly until thickened about 5 minutes.

Once thick, add in vanilla and continue to stir for an additional minute.

Remove from the heat and allow to cool.

Once cool, mix in the coconut and almond flour. Then put in the refrigerator to chill for 10 minutes.

Remove from the fridge and mix again. If the dough is too sticky, add in 1 tablespoon of almond flour until you can form a ball with the dough.

Form 12 balls using your hands with the dough.

In a little bowl, combine coconut sugar and cinnamon.

Roll each ball into the cinnamon-sugar mixture.

Serve and enjoy.

Nutrition:

Calories: 66 Cal

Carbs: 10 g

Proteins: 1 g

Fats: 2 g

269. Raspberry Truffles

Preparation Time: 15 Minutes

Cooking Time: 0

Servings: 36

Ingredients:

2 tbsp. cocoa powder, unsweetened

6 oz. of the followin g:

fresh raspberries, dry

chocolate, bittersweet, finely chopped

coconut milk, full-fat

Directions:

Prepare a cookie sheet with parchment paper and set to the side.

Warm a saucepan over medium heat, and add coconut milk.

Remove from the heat and add the chocolate with a rubber spatula, stirring to melt the chocolate

Once smooth, add the raspberries, 5-8 at a time. Stir to coat.

Using two forks, remove the raspberries from the chocolate sauce, allowing the excess sauce to drop back into the pan. Repeat this step until you have coated all raspberries.

Place the raspberries in the refrigerator for 1 hour or until firm.

In a shallow bowl with a lid, add the cocoa powder.

Once truffles are firm, place 5 to 8 truffles in the bowl and shake to coat with cocoa powder.

Return to the refrigerator until ready to serve.

Nutrition:

Calories: 39 Cal Carbs: 3.8 g

Proteins: 0.6 g

Fats: 2.6 g

270. Pistachio Gelato

Preparation Time: 7 Hr. 60 Minutes

Cooking Time: -

Servings: 4

Ingredients:

½ t. almond extract

1 c. of the following:

Medjool dates

pistachios, unsalted, shells removed

1 big avocado

2 ½ c. cashew milk

Directions:

In a blender, add almond extract, dates, pistachios, avocado, and milk and blend until smooth.

Once smooth, pour into a loaf pan, topping with chopped pistachios and freeze for 8 hours or overnight.

Remove from the freezer and allow to fall for 15 minutes before serving.

Scoop and serve.

Nutrition:

Calories: 345 Cal

Carbs: 38.8 g

Proteins: 6.5 g

Fats: 19.8 g

271. Berry Bites

Preparation Time: 60 Minutes

Cooking Time: 0

Servings: 13

Ingredients:

Dash Himalayan pink salt

1/16 t. stevia

½ t. vanilla

½ c. blackberries

2/3 c. coconut butter

Directions:

In a food processor, add coconut butter, blackberries, vanilla, stevia, and salt; blend until well combined.

Using your hands, form them into 1 ½-inch balls, and place them on parchment a paper on a flat dish.

Place the dish in the freezer for 15 minutes to set.

Store in refrigerator and serve cool.

Nutrition:

Calories: 75 Cal

Carbs: 2.8 g

Proteins: 0.8 g

Fats: 7.2 g

272. Espresso Cups

Preparation Time: 20 Minutes

Cooking Time: 0

Servings: 22

Ingredients:

15 drops vanilla stevia

1 ½ tbsp. instant espresso powder

1 tbsp. coconut milk

2 tbsp. cocoa powder

1/3 c. of the following:

coconut oil

almond butter

Directions:

In a saucepan over medium-low heat, melt the almond butter, coconut oil, coconut powder, coconut milk, espresso powder, and stevia. Stir frequently not to scorch.

Pour into the candy molds or ice cube trays and freeze for 30 minutes.

Store in the refrigerator and serve cool.

Nutrition:

Calories: 77

Carbohydrates: 1 g

Proteins: 1 g

Fats: 8 g

273. Himalayan Raspberry Fat Bombs

Preparation Time: 55 Minutes

Cooking Time: 0

Servings: 4

Ingredients:

3 cups golden Himalayan raspberries

1 tsp vanilla extract

16 oz cream cheese, room temperature

4 tbsp unsalted butter

2 tbsp maple (sugar-free) syrup

Directions:

Line a 12-holed muffin tray with cake liners and set aside.

Pour raspberries, vanilla into a blender, and puree until smooth.

In a small saucepan, over medium heat, melt cream cheese and butter until well-combined.

In a medium bowl, evenly combine raspberry mix, cream cheese mix, and maple syrup. Pour mixture into muffin holes.

Refrigerate for 40 minutes and serve after.

Nutrition:

Calories 227 Cal Fat 14.8g

Carbs 5.2g Fiber 2.1g

Protein 4.68g

274. Stewed Rhubarb

Preparation Time: 10 Minutes

Cooking Time: 7 Hours

Servings: 4

Ingredients:

5 cups rhubarb, chopped

2 tablespoons coconut butter

1/3 cup water

2/3 cup coconut sugar

1 teaspoon vanilla extract

Directions:

Put rhubarb in your slow cooker.

Add water and sugar, stir gently, cover and cook on Lo w for 7 hours.

Add coconut butter and vanilla extract, stir and keep in the fridge until it's cold.

Enjoy!

Nutrition:

Calories: 120 Cal

Fat: 2 g

Fiber: 3 g

Carbs: 6 g

Protein: 1 g

275. Peach Cobbler

Preparation Time: 10 Minutes

Cooking Time: 4 Hours

Servings: 4

Ingredients: ¼ cup coconut sugar

4 cups peaches, peeled and sliced

½ teaspoon cinnamon powder

1 and ½ cups vegan sweet crackers, crushed

¼ cup stevia ¼ teaspoon nutmeg, ground

½ cup almond milk 1 teaspoon vanilla extract

Cooking spray

Directions:

In a bowl, mix peaches with coconut sugar and cinnamon and stir.

In a separate bowl, mix crackers with stevia, nutmeg, almond milk and vanilla extract and stir.

Spray your slow cooker with cooking spray and spread peaches on the bottom.

Add crackers mix, spread, cover and cook on Low for 4 hours.

Divide cobbler between plates and serve.

Enjoy!

Nutrition:

Calories: 212 Cal Fat: 4 g Fiber :4 g

Carbs: 7 g Protein: 3 g

276. Apple Mix

Preparation Time: 10 Minutes

Cooking Time: 4 Hours

Servings: 6

Ingredients:

6 apples, cored, peeled and sliced

1 and ½ cups almond flour

Cooking spray

1 cup coconut sugar

1 tablespoon cinnamon powder

¾ cup cashew butter, melted

Directions:

Add apple slices to your slow cooker after you've greased it with cooking spray

Add flour, sugar, cinnamon and coconut butter, stir gently, cover, cook on High for 4 hours, divide into bowls and serve cold.

Enjoy!

Nutrition:

Calories: 200

Fat: 5

Fiber: 5

Carbs: 8

Protein: 4

277. Poached Plums

Preparation Time: 10 Minutes

Cooking Time: 3 Hours

Servings: 6

Ingredients:

14 plums, halved

1 and ¼ cups coconut sugar

1 teaspoon cinnamon powder

¼ cup water

Directions:

Arrange plums in your slow cooker, add sugar, cinnamon and water, stir, cover, cook on Low for 3 hours, divide into cups and serve cold.

Enjoy!

Nutrition:

Calories: 150 Cal

Fat: 2 g

Fiber: 1 g

Carbs: 2 g

Protein: 3 g

278. Rice Pudding

Preparation Time: 10 Minutes

Cooking Time: 5 Hours

Servings: 4

Ingredients:

6 and ½ cups water

1 cup coconut sugar

2 cups white rice, washed and rinsed

2 cinnamon sticks

½ cup coconut, shredded

Directions:

In your slow cooker, mix water with coconut sugar, rice, cinnamon and coconut, stir, cover and cook on High for 5 hours.

Divide pudding into cups and serve cold.

Enjoy!

Nutrition:

Calories: 213 Cal

Fat: 4 g

Fiber 6 g

Carbs: 9 g

Protein: 4 g

279. Cinnamon Rice

Preparation Time: 10 Minutes

Cooking Time: 35 Minutes

Servings: 4

Ingredients: 3 and ½ cups water

1 cup coconut sugar

2 cups white rice, washed and rinsed

2 cinnamon sticks

½ cup coconut, shredded

Directions:

In your air fryer, mix water with coconut sugar, rice, cinnamon and coconut, stir, cover and cook at 365 degrees F for 35 minutes.

Divide pudding into cups and serve cold.

Enjoy!

Nutrition:

Calories: 213 Cal Fat: 4 g Fiber: 6 g

Carbs: 9 g Protein: 4 g

280. Easy Buns

Preparation Time: 10 Minutes

Cooking Time: 30 Minutes

Servings: 8

Ingredients: ½ cup coconut flour

1/3 cup psyllium husks

2 tablespoons stevia

1 teaspoon baking powder

½ teaspoon cinnamon powder

½ teaspoon cloves, ground

3 tablespoons flax meal combined with 3 tablespoons water

Some chocolate chips, unsweetened

Directions:

In a bowl, mix flour with psyllium husks, swerve, baking powder, salt, cinnamon, cloves and chocolate chips and stir well.

Add water and flax meal, stir well until you obtain a dough, shape 8 buns and arrange them on a lined baking sheet.

Introduce in the air fryer and cook at 350 degrees for 30 minutes.

Serve these buns warm.

Nutri tion:

Calories: 140 Cal Fat: 3 g

Fiber: 3 g Carbs: 7 g Protein: 6 g

281. Zucchini Bread

Preparation Time: 10 Minutes

Cooking Time: 35 Minutes

Servings: 6

Ingredients: 1 cup natural applesauce

1 ½ banana, mashed

1 tablespoon vanilla extract

4 tablespoons coconut sugar

2 cups zucchini, grated

2 and ½ cups coconut flour

½ cup baking cocoa powder

1 teaspoon baking soda

¼ teaspoon baking powder

1 teaspoon cinnamon powder

½ cup walnuts, chopped

Cooking spray

Directions:

Grease a loaf pan with cooking spray, add zucchini, sugar, vanilla, banana, applesauce, flour, cocoa powder, baking soda, baking powder, cinnamon and walnuts, whisk well, introduce in the fryer and cook at 365 degrees F for 35 minutes. Leave the bread to cool down, slice and serve. Enjoy!

Nutrition: Calories: 192 Fat: 3

Fiber: 6 Carbs: 8Protein: 3

282.   Pear Pudding

Preparation Time: 5 Minutes

Cooking Time: 30 Minutes

Servings: 4

Ingredients:

2 cups pears, chopped

2 cups coconut milk

1 tablespoon coconut butter, melted

3 tablespoons stevia

½ teaspoon cinnamon powder

1 cup coconut flakes

½ cup walnuts, chopped

Directions:

In a pudding pan, mix milk with stevia, butter, coconut, cinnamon, pears and walnuts, stir, introduce in your air fryer and cook at 365 degrees F for 30 minutes

Divide into bowls and serve cold.

Enjoy!

Nutrition:

Calories: 202 Cal

Fat: 3 g

Fiber: 4 g

Carbs: 8 g

Protein: 7 g

283.   Cauliflower Pudding

Preparation Time: 10 Minutes

Cooking Time: 30 Minutes

Servings: 4

Ingredients:

2 and ½ cups water

1 cup coconut sugar

2 cups cauliflower rice

2 cinnamon sticks

½ cup coconut, shredded

Directions:

In a pan that fits your air fryer, mix water with coconut sugar, cauliflower rice, cinnamon and coconut, stir, introduce in the fryer and cook at 365 degrees F for 30 minutes

Divide pudding into cups and serve cold.

Enjoy!

Nutrition:

Calories: 203 Cal

Fat: 4 g

Fiber: 6 g

Carbs: 9 g

Protein: 4 g

284. Exuberant Pumpkin Fudge

Preparation Time: 120 Minutes

Cooking Time: 0

Serving: 25

Ingredients 1 and a ¾ cup of coconut butter

1 cup of pumpkin puree

1 teaspoon of ground cinnamon

¼ teaspoon of ground nutmeg

1 tablespoon of coconut oil

Directions Take an 8x8 inch square baking pan and line it with aluminum foil to start with

Take a spoon of the coconut butter and add into a heated pan; let the butter melt over low heat. Toss in the spices and pumpkin and keep stirring it until a grainy texture has formed. Pour in the coconut oil and keep stirring it vigorously in order to make sure that everything is combined nicely. Scoop up the mixture into the previously prepared baking pan and distribute evenly

Place a piece of wax paper over the top of the mixture and p ress on the upper side to make evenly straighten up the topsid. Remove the wax paper and throw it away. Place the mixture in your fridge and let it cool for about 1-2 hours. Take it out and cut it into slices, then eat

Nutrition: Calories: 120 Cal

Protein: 1.2 g   Carbs: 4.2 g   Fats: 10.7 g

285. Bananas and Agave Sauce

Preparation Time: 10 Minutes

Cooking Time: 2 Hours

Servings: 4

Ingredients:

Juice of ½ lemon

3 tablespoons agave nectar

1 tablespoon coconut oil

4 bananas, peeled and sliced diagonally

½ teaspoon cardamom seeds

Directions:

Arrange bananas in your slow cooker, add agave nectar, lemon juice, oil and cardamom, cover and cook on Low for 2 hours.

Divide bananas on plates, drizzle agave sauce all over and serve.

Enjoy!

Nutrition:

Calories: 120 Cal

Fat: 1 g

Fiber: 2 g

Carbs: 8 g

Protein: 3 g

Conclusion

The keto diet has been a lifesaver for many people who have had trouble trying to lose weight using other approaches. The biggest advantage of the keto diet is that you can basically eat until your satisfied. The old problems that plague many diets, such as having to meticulously count calories and watch portion sizes, are all gone. Instead, you can eat to your heart's delight and still lose weight.

One of the problems with the keto diet, from a vegetarian perspective, is the perception that the keto diet is a "meat"-based diet. The fact is, nothing could be further from the truth. The keto diet is actually a fat diet if you can pin one macronutrient on it. Protein is consumed in moderation with the keto diet, rather than being something central to the diet.

As a result of this, the keto diet can be adapted to a vegetarian and even a vegan diet rather easily. Especially in today's world, when protein powders and mixes are widely available, the fact that protein is a moderate part of the keto diet makes it relatively easy to incorporate into a vegetarian lifestyle.

Another reason that the keto diet is easily adapted to the vegetarian lifestyle is that there are many plant sources of heart-healthy fats that make an excellent foundation for the keto diet. You can consume olive oil, palm oil, coconut oil, avocados, and nuts in quantities that will leave you feeling satisfied while setting up a system that will lead to rapid weight loss.

The first step to getting ready for your transformation via the vegetarian keto diet is to take your seven-day shopping list and purchase the items that you need in order to get started. Discipline will be important during the first week. My advice is to consume as much fat as needed and add extra if necessary, so that you don't find yourself feeling unsatisfied or suffering from hunger pangs. If you feel satisfied by consuming large quantities of fats, you will find that you are more likely to stick to the keto diet. One of the mistakes that people make when starting new diets is that they end up cheating on the diet because they are not getting proper levels of nutrients and so become overwhelmed by cravings.

Let's be honest; many of us are going to miss carbohydrates when adopting this diet. So especially during the first week or month of the diet, you might find yourself getting a strong pull to cheat by consuming some bread or pasta. To avoid temptation, find a friend or support group to join you on the diet. By having social support, it will help you to make it through the tough times and not give in to the temptations that you are sure to face from time to time.

Although many people are purists, I recognize the fact that you can occasionally cheat and still stick to the diet for the most part. And in fact, you can do this and have a great deal of success. However, for the first month, you should strictly follow the diet to get a jump start on your weight loss. After this, in my opinion, it is OK to have a once a week cheat day. See what works for you. If you find that doing a cheat day once a week ends up causing problems, then don't use cheat days. However, most people will be able to take one day off per week, and quickly get on track. Don't be neurotic about checking your weight or appearance right after a cheat day. You will probably gain a pound or two back, but that isn't important because, over the course of an entire week, you will find that on the net, you have lost several pounds. The point of a cheat day is so that we are not missing our favorite foods, and it can also serve as a day when we can enjoy social eating with family and friends without making a big deal about our diet. Finally, as I mentioned in the book, when you are following that kind of model, you are more likely to stick with the diet over the long term. And that is the most important part of any diet, being able to stick to it over the long haul. Think in terms of years and decades, rather than dwelling on the effects of one cheat day.

CPSIA information can be obtained
at www.ICGtesting.com
Printed in the USA
LVHW010925011220
673096LV00013B/275